Double Dose

By

Apryl Cox & Aleta Williams

Double Dose © 2013 by Alana's Book Line

Alana's Book Line
www.alanasbookline.org
Lana_books@yahoo.com

First printing in August 2013

ISBN-13: 978-1492225973

ISBN-10: 1492225975

Idea formed by Apryl Cox

Written by Apryl Cox & Aleta L Williams

Cover Designed by Trendsetters Publications

Edited by Gloria Palmer

Dedication

~ Aleta L Williams

This book is dedicated to my three babies—Por'shay, Anthony Jr., and Miracle: Mommy loves her Henderson's babies sooo much!

My mother, Virginia Ann Thomas, and Godmother Cherry: I love and miss you angels dearly!

My husband, father, and my granny—Thanks for everything. I love you all so very much!

~ Apryl Cox

To my baby, the love of my life, my joy, Momma's big lil man, Antwon Tyrese Townsend, everything I do, I do it for you. Thanks for being so understanding. I know this summer we didn't go to Disney or have a whole lot of fun because I stayed stuck in my bed writing or working but you know the blessing that will come out of this. I can't wait to see you on the big screen; your time is coming. Mommy loves you!

To my mother, Marevina Cox aka Mrs. 'I don't play about my baby': LOL. Words can't explain how much I love you, lady. I thank God for you. You are rare; you are one of a kind—so giving, caring, and always, always having my back. I couldn't have asked for a better mother. This is going to take us to the next level. It's on girl; get ready to travel. Wink!

Message from Author Apryl Cox:

Sing with me . . . when I think about the Lord how He saved me, how He raised me, how He filled me with the Holy Ghost, how He healed me to the uttermost . . . when I think about the Lord how He picked me up, turned me around, how He set my feet on solid ground . . . It makes me want to shout hallelujah! Thank you, Jesus! Lord, You're worthy of all the glory, and all the honor, and all the praise! Hallelujah! Thank you, Jesus! Lord, You're worthy of all the glory, and all the honor, and all the praise!

Father God, I want to take this time out to give You all the glory. You are so awesome, sooo awesome. None of this could have ever been done if it weren't for You. Through the tears, aggravation of writing, and then losing what I wrote to have to start all over again, through the days I stayed up late at night and was late for work but You still covered me: Lord, I thank You. I thank You for Your Word that I can do all things through You. I thank You for helping me to complete another project. I thank You for always being there through the good and the bad times. When my days are dark and I'm down in the valley, I thank You for giving me Valley victory. I thank You for loving me when I didn't love myself. I thank You for the push. I even thank You for the red carpet days that are to come. You may not come when I want you to, but You come right on time, and I thank You for that.

I can barely hold it together thinking about this testimony. Just this year I spoke to my spiritual father, Pastor Tom Jones, saying the craziest thing, and as soon as the words came out of my mouth, Lord, You spoke to my heart and I had to correct myself. I told him I don't doubt God, but I doubt myself. Then I heard You say, "The same God that lives in Jesus Christ is the same God that lives on the inside of you, so when you doubt yourself you doubt God."

Everywhere I go, the Lord sends someone to whisper in my ear telling me to "Stop doubting!" Well, I hear You, Lord, and I have made up in my mind to stand on Proverbs 3:5-6, Trust in the Lord with all thy heart and lean not to Apryl's own understanding! I had to make it personal!

Message from *Author Aleta L Williams:*

Father God, I want to say thank you for Jesus. Thank you for removing negative people and unhealthy situations out of my life and replacing them with positivity. I thank you for this vision, and those you have sent my way to help ABL stand tall and bright. God I thank you for everything . . . I love you so much. Lord!!!

Double Dose

By

Apryl Cox & Aleta Williams

Prologue

Nivea was furious when she came out of her bathroom. Von had just hung up in her face without telling her who the female was she'd heard in the background. She knew it wasn't his ghetto-ass baby-momma Coco; she'd know that tramp's voice anywhere. Coco was always extra loud for no reason, and her vocabulary was one that you wouldn't want your children to pick up. The girl was straight ghetto.

The person's voice she'd heard in the background was soft, and she spoke proper English. If she didn't know any better, she would have bet her brand-new Gucci bag that she had heard the voice before, but that was impossible. They didn't know many of the same people, especially not women. *Who in the hell is he with? He'd better not have a female at our spot*, she thought as she walked over to her closet.

Before opening the closet door, she looked at herself in the mirror. She tried to blink away the redness from her tight, slanted eyes that she had grown to love in her adult life. From elementary to junior high school, she was often teased about who she was. Nivea was Asian and black, her five-foot height, one-hundred-ten-pound frame, and tight eyes were inherited from her mother, who was Asian American. However, her full lips and wide hips were handed down to her by her father's mother, a down-south, thick,

1

black beauty. Her perky thirty-six-B-cup boobs and apple-bottom ass she had to credit to Dr. Thomas of Beverly Hills and her husband for such great gifts. Although her handsome husband had thought she was perfect just the way she was, the pouting and fuss that she'd made over wanting the implants had won him over, and he had gone ahead and paid for the surgery as a birthday gift!

"I'm beautiful," Nivea whispered as she pulled her long, jet-black hair into a ponytail and wrapped it in a tight bun. She then glanced over at her sexy, chocolate husband, who was sound asleep. She adored Jay; he was the man of her dreams. Tall, dark, handsome, wealthy, gentle, kind, and he loved and adored her with all his fiber. But there was something missing, something that only one man could give her—brief but unforgettable trips on the wild side.

She had to experience him at least once a week or she would go crazy. The Von experience was like a drug. If she didn't have him, she would begin to have side effects—mood swings. She would even snap and become annoyed with Jay for no reason at all. Out of guilt, she'd tried several times to let him go—cold turkey; but the desire to have him overrode the guilt. Now here she was again, ready to satisfy her addiction. If there was another girl in his presence, she was going to do more than satisfy her addiction. She was going to show him that she would forever be the other woman, and no one would take her place until the two of them were completely over.

Nivea slid open her closet door and walked over to the rack that held her casual wear. She grabbed her white Pink sweat pants, a trademark of Victoria's Secret. She walked over to where her blouses were hanging and grabbed her Pink T-Shirt. She then walked to the back of the closet and grabbed a pair of pink-and-white Puma sneakers. Nivea removed her nightgown and dressed. She intentionally didn't put on a bra or a thong.

When she walked out of the closet, she looked over at Jay, who was still asleep. She thought she'd better not wake him up, but she would text him once she was in the car to let him know that she was at the gym. *This has to stop,* she thought as she walked over to the bedroom door to exit.

"Where are you going," Jay's voice was scratchy when he spoke. He sat up in the bed and looked at the red clock sitting on the nightstand.

Nivea jumped at the sound of her husband's voice, and she turned around slowly to face him. She let out a short breath and cleared her throat.

"It's after midnight, Niv; where are you going?" He turned on the night lamp.

"Umm, to my father's house." She'd changed up her lie just that quickly. She had planned to tell him that she was going to the gym.

"What's the matter with your father? Is everything okay?" He threw the covers off him, preparing to get out the bed.

"Oh no, he's fine, honey. It's just that, well, he's missing my mother again, and he wants me to come over to keep him company. I didn't want to wake you so I had planned to text you once I was in the car."

He looked at her for a minute with a look of confusion. She knew that he wouldn't have wanted to wake up to a text.

"Alright, be safe," he told her, then turned off the lamp. He lay back down in the bed; sleep was far from his mind.

"I love you," Nivea whispered before she walked out of the door in search of another man.

CRSO

In the car, Nivea tried dialing Von's number several times, but he kept sending her to voicemail.

"He is so damn childish," she uttered, tossing the phone on the car floor. Nivea hopped on the freeway and did over eighty mph all the way to the city of Carson. A trip that would normally take seventeen minutes took nine.

As she was driving past his complex, she saw his car pull out of the driveway. She was on the other side of the street, and to be on the same side as he was, she had to go about a block down to make a U-turn. Von was a speed driver. She hoped that she didn't lose him. As she waited on the few cars to past by, she reached for her phone on the floor. He was still sending her to voicemail.

"Von, you need to stop playing with me. Where in the hell are you going and who was that I heard in the background?" She left the message as she followed behind him back to the freeway.

"Wait one damn minute! I know he is not about to pull up in here!" she mumbled to herself when she saw Von slow down as if he was about to turn into a Motel 6. Her heart rate began to speed up, and it felt as if butterflies were having a party in her stomach.

ଓଃ୨୦

She can't resist me, if she wanted to, Von thought as he cracked a smile. When he'd hung up on Nivea, it wasn't because she had heard his lady friend's voice in the background, but because she was playing games. Those guilt trips she was starting to have had been getting on his damn nerves. Fuck that! He was Von—the man! He was like the Jay-Z of Los Angeles County. He didn't need her. He could have had plenty of women, but there was something about *this* woman that made him refuse to let her go. The way she kept calling back-to-back, he knew that she was pissed, but he didn't think that she would leave her house at that time of the morning to come and see him. She never had before.

"She needs to stop playing and keep that shit real," Von blurted out.

"Huh?" Brandy looked at him confused.

Von looked over at her and shook his head as if he hadn't meant anything by his comment. Von parked, cut the car off, and got out. He stood there staring at Brandy as if he didn't see Nivea's black-on-black Rover pull into the parking lot.

"Come on, get out." When Brandy got out, Von quickly grabbed her by the hand and walked toward the room.

"Don't we have to pay?" Brandy asked.

Von ignored her question and continued to walk to room 106. As soon as he put his hand on the knob, a buzzer went off, and Von turned the knob to open the door. He looked at a puzzled Brandy and winked.

CRSO

Nivea, stop with this foolishness. You have a husband at home who loves you dearly. Her conscience began to lecture her, and she slowed her pace, but she never stopped walking toward Von and his chick. The closer she got, the more upset she became. *How dare him!*

Enough with this madness! Your husband loves and takes care of you; you are going to lose him. That was so true. Jay did love her, and if he ever found out about them, he would probably kill them both.

She had come too far to go back. She was there, and she wanted to know what in the hell was going on, who was he with. Von and the chick were now standing in front of the room. When Nivea saw Von open the door, she began to lightly jog their way. Von saw Nivea coming, and pulled Brandy into his arms and kissed her.

Nivea became outraged. *What in the hell is she doing with my man? Did I just say "my?" Yes, I did.*

"TrayVon, what in the hell is your problem, and who in the fuck is this?" Nivea looked at woman he was with, and her expression went from angry to surprised when she recognized who it was. "The fucking nurse?" She turned up her nose and looked Brandy up and down as if she was disgusted. Nivea then looked at

Von. "Like really, Von?" She chuckled. "If you don't send this tired, thirsty bitch home and now . . ." She put her hands on her hips.

Brandy stepped back and gave Nivea a once-over. "Excuse you. You're calling somebody thirsty, and you're the one following a man to a motel, jumping out, acting all crazy? Wait, and don't you have a man? Are you trying to get a double dose? Isn't your husband—"

Before Brandy could finish her sentence, Nivea charged at her and grabbed her hair. Just as Von was pulling Nivea off Brandy, Brandy punched her in the side of the face. Von stepped between them.

"Brandy, go home. I'll call you later."

Brandy looked at him with her eyebrows up.

"Just go."

He reached in his pocket, pulled out a stack, pulled three twenties off, and tried to hand them to Brandy.

"Nigga, I don't need you or your money." She looked over at Nivea, who was standing with her arms folded as if she had won the battle. "Bitch, this ain't over. I will have the last laugh." She shook her head and walked away.

Nivea began yelling and screaming names at Brandy. Brandy turned around and gave her the bird. Nivea went to charge at her, but Von grabbed her by the waist and pulled her into the room.

"Let me go, Von. Now!" she ordered, trying to fight him off her. "I am done with you. Guess I wasn't good enough. You had to run off with the damn nurse?"

Von didn't even bother to respond, He had a way of speaking without even opening his mouth. Von picked her up off her feet and looked into her eyes; Nivea looked away. The look said it all. He was in charge, and he was about to get what he wanted.

Nivea didn't like the fact that she was giving in so easy. "Put me down, Von. I am not playing with you. You no-good, son of a bitch, I said put me down."

Von tossed Nivea on the bed and climbed on top of her. He grabbed each of her arms, pinned them over her head, holding them in place with one hand. He used his other hand to caress her face. "Girl, you know you want this." He smiled as he used his knee to pry her legs open.

"Fuck you! I don't want you. Go, call that bitch back because you will not get any of this."

Nivea's mouth was saying one thing, but he knew what she wanted and he wanted her, too. Still holding her arms above her head, Von began to kiss and bite on her neck while grinding in a slow circular motion. Between feeling Von's full, throbbing erection pressing against her love box and the passionate kisses he planted on her neck, her "no's" changed into moans of pure bliss.

Nivea instantly became moist, and Von knew he had her. As his tongue found hers, he continued his grind for a few more minutes until he was sure that she was calm. Then he let her arms go and stood up from the bed. Licking his lips, he eyed her seductively.

Nivea watched as Von began to remove his clothes. Damn! Clothes on or off, everything about him screamed, "Sexy muthafucka!" To her, his body was sculptured like a fine piece of art, one that would be considered a masterpiece to many. He turned her on so much, Nivea couldn't help but place her fingers in her mouth, getting them nice and wet; and then she slid them in her most sensitive hot spot. "Mmmm," she moaned as she licked her lips and teased her pearl tongue.

When he was done undressing, he pulled off Nivea's shoes, then her pants. "Damn!" he mumbled as he eyed her golden flesh. He stood there for a minute, taking her all in; a slight tremor ran through her body, caused by the way Von looked at her. His stare was intoxicating. His eyes told her that he was about to do damage, and she surrendered every inch of her body, mind, and soul to him. He took Nivea's creamy hand and placed her fingers in his mouth, sucking all her juices off them. After sucking them clean, he was ready for his appetizer. Von pulled Nivea to the edge of the bed, lowered himself between her thighs, and began to feast on her, making tingling, swirling motion inside her. Von slurped and sucked her to the end of no return; Nivea flooded a river twice.

"Turn over," he commanded, and she got into his favorite position—doggy style. He slowly entered her, burying himself deep inside of her, and brought his manhood to full measure. He began to stroke her faster, plunging himself in her just the way she liked it. Hearing her cry out in pleasure caused him to grow a few more inches.

"Vonnnn, yessss," she hollered as she gripped the sheets on the bed and threw it back to meet his next powerfully thrust.

"Tell him you miss him," Von said, speaking of his ten inches as he went deeper, hitting her G-spot.

"Yessss, baby, I missed you. Ohhhh yessss…Tell me you're sorry," he said, twisting his body a little, slightly bending his leg, and gripping her hip to punish her with a possessive thrust.

It was painful but at the same time felt too damn good. She thought she would lose her mind.

"Tell me you're sorry; tell me you're going to act right." He began to pound in and out of her with more force.

"Da . . . daddy, I'm, sorrrryyyy, ooooh!" she screamed, on the verge of exploding.

"Damn, baby, this pussy is wet for daddy, ain't it?" Von's eyes were closed and his head leaned back as he continued to beat it up. "Tell daddy what you want him to do, girl . . ."

"Ohhhh, cummmm with me, daddy . . ."

Von tried to go deeper as he was beating up her insides. She locked up her muscles on his bare flesh and arched her back, bucking on him as they both collided in perfect rhythm.

"Oh shit . . . Oh shit . . ." Von was there. He grabbed Nivea's ass so she couldn't move, and they both released long and hard as Nivea cried out, enjoying the feeling of his warm seed spilling inside of her.

"Mmmm, daddy . . ."

She was spent. She lay out on the bed and Von collapsed on top of her. He rolled over on his back, pulling Nivea in his arms as she lay there thinking. *How did I get here? How did I let this go this far?* She cuddled up closer in his arms, and right before she dozed off, she thought, *Is it possible to love my husband and his twin brother?*

Chapter One ~ Four Months Earlier

TraVon and Coco

It is crazy stupid how a person deals with the same bullshit over and over again. It's as if they know the person or situation isn't adding any positivity to their life, but yet and still, they refuse to let go. They prefer to sulk in disappointment after disappointment and heartbreak after heartbreak, hoping that the best is yct to come.

"I'm so sick of your shit TrayVon Deeds. I'm fucking tired," Coco fussed as she paced back and forth in front of the living room window waiting for Von, her man of three years and her baby-daddy to pull up. She was pissed when she'd awakened this morning and his ass wasn't in bed. She'd bribed her cousin to watch Little Von so they could have some me time, and his ass never showed up. "This nigga really thinks I'm going to put up with his shit forever," she continued, still pacing back and forth. "One day . . . one day, I promise I'm going to leave his lying ass."

When Coco saw Von's truck pull into the driveway, she stormed over to the front door and snatched it open. Von didn't even step both feet out of the truck good before Coco went in on him. "Hurry up and bring that ass in here before I give the neighbors a show." Coco was threatening to act a fool. Although she wasn't trying to have her neighbors all up in her business, she would have just to piss Von off; he hated a lot of attention. She crossed her arms over her chest and tapped her feet with anticipation. Coco was ready to jump all over his ass as soon as he walked into the door.

He we go, Von thought as he rubbed his hands across his face, regretting coming home. *I should have stayed where I was until later. It's too early for this shit.* Von walked into the house, past Coco. She was right behind him.

"Oh so you're just going to walk up in here like you're the king or some shit?"

"I am," he answered, he took his shirt off, and tossed it on the sofa.

"What you taking off your shirt for? I hope you don't think you're about to lie down."

Von stopped in mid-stride, with one hand on the stair rail; he turned and looked at her. "So you mean I can't come in my house and take off my clothes? What's the fucking problem? A nigga's tired," he complained.

"I don't give a damn how tired you are. You're going to take my ass somewhere this morning. You been gone all yesterday, then bring your ass up in here like you owe me nothing. I told you I was letting Apple watch the baby and that I wanted to kick it, but what do you do? The same shit you always do: Say fuck me and my feelings, and do you and whatever hoe you're sleeping with.'

"Why a bitch always gotta be involved? A nigga's hustlin', damn!" Von turned and went up the steps, and Coco followed behind him.

"So you're just going to walk away like that?"

"I'm tired Co, and I don't have time for your drama, so chill with all that shit." He turned and looked up at her with a mean glare, hoping to shut her up, but she wasn't having it. She was pissed and he was going to make it right.

"Please, nigga, tired of what? Only a bird-brain, Barbie bitch would believe you've only been in the streets hustlin' all night. You are not about to keep treating me like a sideline hoe; you got me all the way fucked up." She placed her hands on her hips. "Now, I'm ready to go."

Coco went on and on fussing in his ear until he finally gave in. He knew he had been neglecting her, but the street was demanding a lot of his time, and Coco nagged too damn much.

'Gotdamn, Co, let's go." Von went into the closet, grabbed a blue polo shirt, and put it on.

Twirling her neck as only she could, Coco pouted, "Why in the hell you have to say it like that? What, you don't want to take me to breakfast? Damn, can a bitch get a happy meal or something? I know you trick on them ratchet bitches you're fucking."

This bitch done gave me a migraine. Von shook his head at the words coming out of Coco's mouth. "I'll be in the truck and hurry up." He turned and left her standing there.

Coco threw on some jeans, a sweater, and her flip-flops. Although she still wasn't satisfied, she was going because she knew he didn't want to. She was getting her way; that was all that mattered. "That's what I thought," she said to herself. She took off her headscarf and combed down her blonde wrap. When she was done, she grabbed her purse and her cell, and left out the house.

Inside the truck, Coco went into detective mode. She sniffed the air as her eyes scanned the truck for any signs of females. *Yeah, he thinks I'm stupid. I know he hasn't been in the streets all night. He slept some damn where, at some bitch's house! Now he wants to bring his ass home and sleep. When do I get any time?*

She turned and looked out of the window. *I know the fight is tonight, and he ain't trying to take me. That's why his ass is taking me out.* Coco thought about calling him out on it, but changed her mind. She was focusing on the current issue at hand. Coco's mind was on overdrive. Dealing with Von always had her like that. He'd cheated, disrespected, and neglected her for so long she couldn't remember the last time, or the first time, that she could say that he'd actually made her happy. No matter how miserable she was, she stayed; and because he made her unhappy, her nagging and fussing were to make him feel what she felt.

The twenty-minute ride to Roscoe's Chicken and Waffles was silent until they pulled into the restaurant parking lot. "I don't like this one, you know that. Let's go to the one on Pico." Coco looked at Von while she waited for his response.

"They're all the same." Von pulled into a parking space right in front of the door. He killed the engine on the truck and jumped out.

Coco sat there with her arms folded as she watched him walk into the restaurant. She waited a few minutes to see if he would come back out for her, but when she saw him through the window, being escorted to a table by some chick with a big smile on her face, she grabbed her purse and hurriedly jumped out the truck.

"Fuck," Coco griped as she walked inside to the table, "so you were just going to leave me in the truck so you could have the next bitch smiling in your face? What, you know her? Is that's why you wanted to come here?" As Coco flopped down in her seat, she turned and looked at the waitress and her name badge. "Chell, is it your job to flirt with the customers or is it your job to serve us?"

Chell looked at Von, then looked back at Coco. "I'll be back to take your order," she said and walked away.

"Why you always gotta act stupid?" Von shook his head at her. He picked up the menu and looked it over.

"Why you always gotta be smiling all up in a bitch's face?"

"Whatever man," he shined her on.

"Oh, so now you're mad? Nigga, if that was me, you'd have a straight attitude."

"Bitches get attitudes," was his response.

"Real funny, Von, but it's cool." Coco watched Von continue to stare at the menu as if he didn't know what he wanted. He knew Roscoe's menu like the back of his hand, and the Obama special was what he always ordered.

A few minutes later, the waitress walked back over. She purposely looked at Von, and asked if he was ready to order. Before Von could respond, Coco went off.

"Let me tell your freckle-face ass something. When you serve a woman," Coco pointed to her chest, "and her man," she pointed at Von, "out of respect, you address the lady of the table, because that shit that you think you're doing will get you fucked up."

This bitch doesn't know that I will take her man and beat her ass. She'd better be glad I need this job.

Von was tired of her shit and he knew he had to get her out of there before she acted a plum fool. Coco was a straight fool. No matter where he took her, if a female looked at him wrong, he either had to be fucking her, had fucked her, or was trying to fuck her. In her book, he was guilty by association.

"Coco, cut that shit out. You know what? Let's just order to go. Let me get two Obama specials and two lemonades."

Chell gave Von a nod and walked off. "Your orders will be at the front," she said over her shoulder.

"Oh, so now we have to go? You know what? I don't even want the shit no more!"

Von didn't say anything. He simply got up from his seat and went to the front to wait for their order. He couldn't wait to pay and get her the hell up out of there.

It took about ten minutes before the cashier called their order. Von hurriedly got up and paid for the food. On their way to the door, the waitress was standing by the counter. Coco stopped and faced her. "Here's a tip: nobody's riding that black stallion but me," she pointed her finger at her chest. "Next time, think twice before you try to be extra friendly with mines." She then gave her the once over. "You're not his type," Coco clowned before walking out of the door.

She is so insecure, thought the waitress. *Looks don't mean anything. It's all about how you feel about yourself.*

Coco was hood no doubt; not only did she have that ghetto 'tude, but she had the look to match. She stayed rocking long, acrylic fingernails with designs that matched her toenails. Her blond weave touched the bottom of her back, but it looked good with her light-brown skin. She was short, with a nice, plump butt and her thirty-six-B cup fit her just right. Dudes stayed trying to holla. Except for one, she wouldn't give them the time of the day. Von was the one she wanted to desire her. All she had to do was say the words, 'I'm ready,' and she would have the love she yearned for, but she couldn't get Von out of her system no matter how doggish he was.

"You feel better now?" Von asked when she got in the car.

"Whatever," she rolled her eyes.

Von leaned over and pulled her into his arms. "I know what you need, and I am going to give it to you when we get home." He tried kissing her, and Coco pretended she was trying to push him away.

"Mooove," she cooed.

Von slid his hand between her legs. "Why did you wear these tight-ass jeans? I could have got me some right here." He began to suck on her neck.

"You should have come home last night, and you would have got this and more." Coco rubbed his head. She looked over to the window to see if the waitress was looking and, sure enough, the bitch was. Coco didn't even bother to say anything; she just chuckled to herself.

"What are you laughing at?" Von lifted up.

"Nothing. Let's go," she said, now all hot and bothered.

"Hold up, baby, let me go take a piss." He grabbed himself. "I'll be right back." Von opened the door and got out.

"You better hurry up, too," Coco went along with Von's bull.

She knew his ass all too well, and she knew he was up to something. Coco waited a few minutes, then got out. All it took was for her to see the waitress come from the area of the bathrooms.

"Bitch, didn't I just for warn you about that one?" Coco charged at her, but Von grabbed her around the waist.

"Man, chill out, why are you tripping?"

"Wait a minute, you insecure bitch? You got me all the way mixed up." Chell took off her apron and tossed it on the floor. "What you wanna do?" She threw up her guards, ready to square off. "Let your rat go," Chell challenged.

"Let me the fuck go, Von," Coco was pissed.

Chell charged at Coco and began to throw wild blows. She was only inches away from tagging Coco in the face when her boss ran over and grabbed her.

"Please leave," the restaurant manager asked Von. Chell was still trying to break away from the short, chubby guy, but he had a grip on her. Coco was going crazy as Von tried to force her out the door. She grabbed the first thing she saw—the ketchup bottle—and hurled it toward Chell. Then she grabbed the napkin holder, but before she could get it in the air, Von snatched in from her. He picked her up, tossed her over his shoulder, and left out.

"Get your ass in the truck. You're crazy." He tossed her in the truck and slammed her door. He then ran over and got in on his side.

As soon as he got in, she drew her hand back, slapped the taste out of his mouth, and began swinging on him,

"You scandalous nigga, you ain't shit!" She continued to try to hit him, cursing and yelling in the interim.

Von grabbed her arms. "Coco, stop tripping. Nobody was trying to talk to that girl. Why are you acting stupid?"

"Nigga, fuck you, I ain't stupid." She tried to break away from his grip but it was too tight. "I hate you. I hate you. You ain't shit."

"Coco, you'd better stop tripping. I went to take a piss. That girl was coming from the back at the same time I left out of the restroom. You know damn well I ain't about to talk to a bitch while you out here."

"But you do talk to bitches?"

"There you go putting words in my mouth. Coco, stop tripping. Ain't nobody trying to talk to that girl!" He looked her in her eye, "You hear me, man?"

"Just take me home." She turned her head and looked out of the window.

Von let her go. "You're crazy, girl," he laughed then started the truck and pulled off. "You know damn well I wouldn't be in there talking to no bitch and your crazy ass is out here. You be tripping."

"Just stop talking to me; leave me alone." Coco folded her arms. "I am so tired of your shit."

"I love you, too," was his reply.

When Von pulled into their driveway, Coco jumped out of the truck and hurried in the house. Von grabbed the food and went in right behind her. As he walked in the door, he saw Coco running up the stairs. He put the food in the kitchen, and when he got upstairs to their room, Coco had taking off her pants and was lying on her side of the bed. Von stood there for a second, looking at her. He knew she was pissed, but he had just what she needed to make her feel better. He quickly undressed and climbed on top of her.

"Move, Von, I don't have time." She pushed him.

Coco moved her head from side to side. "Get off me, please. I'm good." She was exhausted and frustrated with Von.

Von didn't say a thing. He grabbed his thick and hard member. As he began to rub it up and down Coco's nookie, she began to get wet. Coco opened her legs and Von slid inside of her. Von began to stroke her long and slow, rotating his hips, making sure he hit her walls. "Damn, Co, I love this shit, girl." He continued to hit each wall.

"Baby, right there," Coco cooed, "right there, Von . . ."

For the next hour, the two pleased each other the only way they knew how—with hot and steamy sex. When Von was done, Coco was sleeping like a baby. Von got up and showered. He called Coco's cousin and told her he was coming to get the baby. When he got back he, the baby, and Coco enjoyed chicken and waffles in bed.

CRSO

JayVon

Sitting behind his cherry oak desk, JayVon pressed the black button on the intercom and spoke into it. "Stephanie," he called for his assistant.

"Yes, Mr. Deeds?" Stephanie replied as she continued to look on the Internet at the different prices the spa offered.

"Hold all of my calls and get my wife on line two, please."

"Sure, Mr. Deeds, I will put her right through when I get her on the line."

"Thanks, Stephanie."

JayVon released the intercom and continued typing on his laptop, closing up a deal he'd made on a three-story, seven-bedroom mini-mansion. It had been on the market for several months, and he'd finally found not only the couple with enough money to purchase the home, but their personalities would fit right in with the other stuck-up neighbors. After sending out a few emails confirming that the mansion was now sold, he shut his laptop, reclined back in his executive leather, black chair, and propped his feet up on his desk. With his eyes closed, he loosened his tie, wiggled it from around his neck, and unbuttoned the top button on his shirt. He needed a few minutes to relax. He had been working nonstop since he had arrived at work twelve hours ago.

As Jay was relaxing, an icky feeling came across him, and his eyes popped open. Jay stared out the large picture window that overlooked the busy Los Angeles city, and he thought of his brother Von. He wondered what he was up to; he prayed that he wasn't in any kind of trouble.

The two, TrayVon (Von) and JayVon (Jay), were so much alike. Identical twins, they could sense when something wasn't right with the other. Although they were close, they were very different—like day and night. His brother loved and lived for the street life, but not Jay. They had been forced into the game by their father when they were just teens.

Unlike his brother, Jay didn't think hustling was that important. He would rather have his head in somebody's books, trying to figure out the formula to an algebra problem, than to ride up and down the block, dropping off cocaine to different trap houses. Although he wasn't a hustler, he'd had no choice. Living with his father, it was a requirement not an option. So what he had done was go to school during the day and hustle at night.

Thanks to his belated grandmother, he'd learned that the art of saving was a valued tool. Unlike Von, who'd spent his money on cars, shoes, clothes, and tricking on different chicks, Jay had stacked his money in the bank and paid his way through college. Eventually he'd flipped that dirty money into a clean investment, "Good Deed Real Estate," with his brother as his silent partner.

He often wondered if his deceased father would have been proud of his choices. Their father had been murdered on the same day that the two had graduated from high school. He didn't even get a chance to see them walk across the stage. The day his father had been murdered, he'd had a feeling something bad was about to happen. It was that same icky feeling that he had now.

Jay reached for the phone on the desk. He was going to call to check on his brother; he wanted to tell him that they needed to set up a time, just the two of them, to talk. They were reaching thirty, and he thought now was a good time for his brother to get out of the game.

"Mr. Deeds?" Stephanie perky voice came through the intercom.

"Yes, Stephanie?

"You have a call on line one."

"I thought I asked you to hold all of my calls, and get my wife on line two?" He was a little annoyed. He got like that when that nasty feeling came about.

"You did, sir, and I am still working on that. She isn't answering the house phone or her cell." To lighten the mood, she added in a more cheerful tone, "But the guy on line one said that, if I don't put him through, he was going to bust a cap in my ass. And, Mr. Deeds, I need the little handful I have." She giggled.

Knowing that could only be one person talking shit and threatening his assistant, he laughed. "Put him through, Stephanie, and please continue to try to reach my wife.

"Will do, sir, and no problem. I will call again as soon as I put Mr. Von through." She then transferred the call.

Instead of talking on the speaker, Jay picked up the phone. "Yo, who is the nigga calling my place of business, making threats?" Jay laughed again.

"Nigga, I heard you're walking around town trying to be me. Niggas say you been dressing like me and even looking like me. What's next, you going to try to take my bitch?"

"If you're talking about Coco's crazy butt, noooo . . . Besides, I got a bad half-Asian and half-black cutie who I'm addicted to. And, what do you mean, I'm trying to be like you? boy, never that. Get your weight up and just maybe."

"My weight? So what are you saying? We're playing big bank take little bank? I don't mind a little extra change in my pocket."

In unison, they burst into a hearty laugh. They were cool like that. They could joke and chill with one another all day. Their bond was sweet.

"S'up? What's good?" Jay asked, breaking the laughter.

"Shit! Just trying to see if we're still on for the fight tonight?"

"Yeah, I'm about to finish up in here in the next hour, then I'll be headed home."

"A'ight. Do I need to bring anything?"

"Nope, just yourself. Nivea is cooking dinner tonight."

Von burst into laughter. Jay ignored his diss. He knew his baby wasn't a good cook, but at least she was trying. The two brothers ended the call with, "Be safe and I love you."

When Jay hung up with his brother, he cursed himself for forgetting to tell him that he wanted to talk to him about making a change. *I will let him know what's up tonight at the party,* he thought.

CR80

Another hour-and-a-half had gone by and his assistant still hadn't gotten hold of his wife. He decided to call it a night and head home; he would try to reach her in the car. He grabbed his briefcase and jacket from the coat rack, and made his way out of the office.

"I still haven't been able to reach her, Mr. Deeds."

Stephanie looked away from her computer screen and up at her handsome boss. Stephanie has been married for three good years. Her husband was her everything, and although she'd never considered dating outside of the Irish race or cheating on her husband, she believed if the opportunity was presented, she would take it there with Mr. Deeds. Just once, she smiled to herself, thinking about the famous saying that had been going around since before time: "Once you go black, you'll never go back." She wondered if it was true.

She looked her boss up and down. He wore a chocolate button-up shirt with a black-and-cream tie to match the suit jacket he was holding over his right shoulder. The black slacks he wore fit him just right, showing off the bulge in his pants. Mr. Deeds was always dressed to impress, and although jewelry to her was too flashy, her boss wore it with class. Jay rocked two diamond studs that were designed as dice. She'd asked, "Why the dice?" He'd told her that, "Life's a gamble, but by the grace of God, my luck hasn't run out yet." That's why the dice in his ears displayed seven spots. He didn't wear a chain, but he did rock a nice link bracelet covered in diamond clusters. The only ring he wore was his wedding ring.

"Stephanie, are you listening to me?" He smiled, knowing that his assistant had an innocent crush on him. He would never cheat on his wife and if, that was if, he ever slipped up, he doubted that it would be with Stephanie. She reminded him of the teacher from the *Little House of Prairie.*

"I'm sorry. I was thinking about something." Stephanie blinked twice, trying to get the lustful thoughts out of her head.

"I've got the fight. You and your husband are welcome to come by the house and watch it with us."

She smiled. Her boss was so cool.

"Before you make a decision, I must let you know that my brother will be there." He laughed and so did she.

Stephanie thought about how he and his brother looked so much alike, yet they were so different. However, they both were alright with her.

"I think we may pass. The mister isn't feeling so good, so he may just want to stay home and watch."

Jay shrugged his shoulders. "Alright." He flashed her signature smile and walked off.

Nice ass, Stephanie thought.

Chapter Two

Jay and Nivea

As Jay pulled his all-white Jag into traffic, he placed a call to his wife. Nivea answered on the first ring.

"Hey, honey."

Jay immediately noticed the frustration in her voice. He already knew where it was coming from. "Baby, we can order Wing Stop." He knew how frustrated she got when it came to cooking; in fact, she wasn't very good at it.

"Honey, my having to cook isn't the reason I'm frustrated. In fact, I'm excited to see what you think of my fried chicken. I have a new recipe," she said as she looked in her basket at the Shake 'N Bake box. "It's Shake 'N Bake."

'Good, I can't wait to taste it." He briefly thought about seeing the Shake 'N Bake commercials as a kid, then he focused back on the issue at hand. "Baby, what is it that has you frustrated?"

"It's the people we're having over for company, that's all."

She began to push her basket down the frozen-food aisle. She stopped right in front of the Stouffer's section, and as she was searching the freezer for the macaroni and cheese, she continued, "Sometimes I get scared and think maybe Von or one of his men is being followed. You know what your brother and his friends are into. They may be after him and his crew, and end up shooting up our house or, worse, kill us." Nivea grabbed two of the family-size boxes of macaroni and cheese, and placed them in her basket. She stood where she was, waiting on Jay to respond.

Jay didn't say anything. He directed his attention to the woman who was walking her dog in the intersection. Jay had learned to block Nivea out. He did that to prevent them from having an argument; he hated to argue. Although there was plenty of truth in what she was saying, he wasn't going to admit it to her. After all, that was his twin brother. Just as he wouldn't bad mouth Nivea's flaws to his brother, he wasn't going to bad mouth his brother's lifestyle to his wife. They both meant the world to him. As Jay made a right onto the freeway ramp, he continued to allow Nivea to vent for just a few minutes more.

She added, "And them gold diggers, or should I say hoodrats, they call dates? Ugh! But that's your family and your friends. I'm just the wife."

Jay cracked a smile at her sarcasm. "Alright, baby. This 405 is bumper-to-bumper. I'm about to listen to some jazz. I'll see you in a bit."

"Ok," she said dryly, "you know the routine."

Jay and Nivea always debated on who would hang up first. They both counted, "One, two . . ." and on three, they released the line. As Nivea put her phone in her purse, she smiled and thought about how much she loved him.

ᚱᛞᚱᛞ

Nivea and Jay had met their freshman year in college. It was love at first sight. She couldn't ask for a better man. He was like a modern-day Romeo. Any woman would die to call him hers. She was uncertain about taking his hand in marriage after he'd revealed to her that his deceased father was a big-time hustler, and his twin brother had taken over the family empire. She was scared. She'd seen enough movies and read plenty of books on the pros and cons of being a hustler's wife. But Jay had proved that he was different. He'd gotten out of the game and made "it do what it do" the respectable way. Now Von, on the other hand, was the opposite. He was what Nivea called triple-H—a hoe, a hustler, and a headache." He so got on her nerves.

ᚱᛞᚱᛞ

Across Town in the City of Cerritos

Coco stood at the door watching Von check himself in the mirror. Von wore black baggy jeans and a red-and-blue throwback Clippers' jersey. The cornrows, phat chain, and Rolex watch he wore made him look like a gangster rapper.

"Where are you going?" she asked, turning up her lip.

Without looking at her, he responded, "To watch the fight; why?" He brushed passed her, walked over to his son, and picked him up from the crib. Little Von was the best thing that had come out of his and Coco's relationship. He would admit that he loved the girl, but he wasn't in love with her, and hated her nagging and ghetto ways.

"Don't wake him up; you ain't going to be here to keep him company," she fussed, trying to take the baby from his arms.

"Man, move." He gave her a look that said he wasn't playing and she backed up. Von kissed his son on the top of the head and laid him back in his crib. "He's getting big. I can't believe he's almost two," he said, more to himself than to Coco.

"They do grow up fast. If you spend more time with us, you won't miss it." She rolled her eyes in the top of her head.

"Be quiet sometimes."

Von walked out of the room. He lightly jogged down the steps that led to the living room. He went to his stash in the floor behind his plant and grabbed his gun, tucking it in his waist. He headed for the door. He couldn't wait to scoop up the cutie he'd met at Starbuck's earlier that day.

"Well, damn, no kiss, no bye, no nothing?" Coco stood there with one hand on her hip.

"Come here, cream puff." Von pulled her into his arms and planted a kiss on her nose then her lips.

This nigga is full of shit, thought Coco.

"Von, can I ask you something?" she pulled away and looked up at him.

"What's up," he asked as he grabbed his L.A. hat off the rack and put it on his head.

"Why didn't you invite me to watch the fight with you?"

"Because I don't even know where I'm watching it and, more than likely, wherever I go will not be a place for children. Stay your ass home. Call some of your homegirls, and y'all have your own little fight party."

"You know you're going to Jay's house, so stop fronting."
She placed her hands on her hips.

"No, I'm not, and if I was, you don't like his wife, so why
would I invite you? You're always starting shit. But I ain't going
over there." He hit her on the ass, turned, and walked out the door.

"I'm so sick of his ass, I swear." Coco stormed out of the
living room and back up the stairs. She flopped down on the bed
and folded her arms.

Damn, I wish I didn't have any children. I wish I would have
never let this nigga get me caught up in his web, she thought as she
stared in a daze, wondering whom she could pay to babysit.

CRSO

Back at JayVon and Nivea's

Nivea was in the kitchen, reading the instructions on the back
of the Shake 'N Bake box, when Jay crept up behind her, wrapped
his arms around her waist, and planted a kiss on the top of her
head.

"Hey, baby."

She turned around to give him a kiss on those juicy lips that
she loved so much. "We're having company. Why are you dressed

in sweats and a T-shirt?" She twitched her lips. "And wait a minute, since when did you start wearing hats?" She stared at his red hat with 'Mayweather' written across the front.

"Niv, I am in my house, and I am comfortable with what I have on." He pulled his hat further down on his head, "And my hat represents the champ. You feel me?"

Every time his brother comes around, he becomes this wanna-be thug.

Jay looked Nivea up and down; as always, she was looking sexy. She wore a pair of leggings with a nice gold blouse that hung off her shoulders and a pair of gold, heeled sandals.

"You look nice," he complimented her.

"Thanks, baby, and you look like a sexy thug," she teased and kissed him.

They were sharing a long, passionate kiss when the doorbell rang. Nivea was the first to break their kiss, letting out a frustrating breath. "Go answer the door." She turned around to finish preparing dinner.

"Baby, should I take these out with me?" Jay asked, referring to the platter she had sitting on the counter. *Her and these damn California rolls. Niggas ain't trying to eat that.*

"Yes, baby, and there's another platter in the fridge. I know the gangsters may not want to try something different, so I have one with meat, crackers, and cheese. I only made that in case there was some hope for them, and they wanted to step out of their element."

"Be nice," was all Jay said. He went to the fridge grabbed the other tray and headed toward the living room.

Jay placed the platters on the table and went to open the door. "What up?" Jay gave dap to his brother first, then their cousin Travis. "How are you, ladies," he addressed the two women who were with them. They both replied that they were fine. Since neither Von nor Travis took it upon himself to introduce the women, he asked each of their names. The short, light-skinned girl with jet-black hair was Tammy; she was with Von. The other tall, brown-skinned girl was Larea; she was with Travis.

"Would you ladies like a beer or something harder?" He looked over at Travis and Von's rude asses. They were eating from the meat and cheese platter.

"I'll take a beer," said Tammy, and went and sat on the couch.

"I'll take one as well," Larea added as she sat on the other couch.

"My wife is cooking. She will be out in a little bit," he told the women. They both shook their heads to say o.k.

The doorbell rang again and Jay answered it. This time it was Boo, Jay, and Ray-Ray; they were brothers. They looked so much alike (big, black, and ugly) that people thought they were triplets, but they weren't. Jay welcomed them in the house and everyone began to interact in some kind of way.

Jay looked over at Von, who was at the bar making himself a drink. He walked up to him and asked, "How's my nephew?"

Von took a sip from the glass of Patron and gave a slight nod. "He's good; getting big as ever."

Jay smiled; he loved children and his nephew even more. Nivea and Jay had found out last year that he couldn't give her a baby. They were considering adoption one day.

"How about on Sunday, the three of us go hang out and shoot some ball? I need to talk to you about something."

Von looked at his brother; he could sense that something was bothering him. Besides not being able to have children, Jay's life was straight. He was always happy and calm. The only time he stressed or got upset was when Von was being reckless, getting in trouble and stuff.

"Sunday is cool." He took another sip of his drink. Jay looked over at Tammy, who was watching one of the undercard fights, then back at his brother.

"Where is Coco? Why don't you ever bring her out?"

"Coco is at the pad where she needs to be."

"Why didn't you bring her?" Jay wasn't a Coco fan, but he didn't dislike her either. Apart from being loud and ghetto at times, she was cool. He would always respect her because she loved his brother's dirty drawers, despite the way he treated her; plus, she was his nephew's mother.

"Man, stop playing," Von laughed.

Jay just shook his head at his brother. He didn't believe that he would ever be with just one woman. "You are a mess, man. Let me run to the restroom." Jay walked off.

Von decided to go in the kitchen to see what Nivea was up to. He knew she didn't care for him, but he liked to mess with her.

CRESO

Coco stood with her baby in her arms, waiting for her neighbor to answer the door. She'd called the twenty-one-year old right after Von had left and offered her fifty bucks to babysit Little Von for a few hours.

"Awwww, give him here," said the babysitter when she answered the door. She reached out her arms, and Coco handed over the baby, then his diaper bag.

"Thanks, Sasha, you are a life saver. Tell your mom I said thanks, too." Sasha was visiting from college.

"Will do. Now go and have fun," she told her. Sasha smiled as she watched Coco walk off looking like a sexy video girl.

As Coco hopped in her truck, her phone rang.

"Hey, B, what's up?" Coco smiled in the phone.

"Nothing, girl, I was wondering if you had anything planned tonight?"

Brandy was dry. She always sounded like that; that's why Coco never really wanted to hang around her. She stayed depressed.

"You mean to tell me that you aren't going in for overtime?" Coco asked.

Coco turned on her windshield wipers; it was beginning to sprinkle. Brandy was forever working double shifts as a nurse over at the county hospital. When she wasn't working, she was dying to get out of the house. Brandy was very private, so she had no idea what was going on in her personal life, but she did know that her nigga didn't work.

"I really wanted to get out tonight."

"Von and I are about to go over to his brother's to watch the fight. You should have called earlier. I probably could have convinced his overprotective ass to let me out of his sight." She laughed. "I would invite you, but that stuck-up wife of his brother's be tripping. We can probably hang out tomorrow, though."

Brandy sighed. "Ok, just let me know. I guess I will go in and do some overtime."

"Alright, I am pulling up to one of Von's spots now. Let me get off this phone."

"Have fun; bye, girl."

She and Brandy hung up. Coco turned up the volume on her Bose and sang along with Keisha Cole, *Enough of No Love,* all the way to Jay's house. She knew Von had to be there.

CR&O

Back at JayVon & Nivea's

Von walked in the kitchen, sniffing in the air. "I don't smell anything. What is that you're cooking?" He walked over and stood next to Nivea where she was standing at the counter, tossing the salad.

"For your information, I am baking chicken. Now why are you in my kitchen?" She threw her hands in the air.

"Baking chicken? We want something fried and greasy; that takes too long." He looked around the kitchen for something to sample. That's when he noticed the box of Shake 'N Bake and the Stouffer's box of macaroni and cheese on the counter. He burst into laughter.

Nivea was looking at him as if he was stupid. She shook her head, thinking that he was high. "The drugs are frying your brain cells."

"At least it knows how to fry." He walked over, grabbed the box, and held it up. "Throw this shit away. Get you some flour, some seasoned salt, and black pepper, and fry us some chicken. Should I show you how?"

Nivea walked over and snatched the box from him. "I don't need your help. I'm baking for my husband and me. It's healthier. If you want fried, I can give you that."

"Yeah, you do that, but let me show you what you need to get started." Von grabbed a pan from the cabinet, the flour, and some cooking oil. He placed the cooking oil in the skillet, sat it on a burner on the stove, and turned on the fire. "Season your chicken, then put some flour on it. When the grease gets hot, put the chicken in the pan. Don't burn the shit."

Nivea screamed, "Jay, come and get your annoying brother."

Jay was already on his way in the kitchen when she'd called him. "What's going on in here?" he asked, standing in the doorway.

"Get him out of my kitchen. Now!" She turned her back on them both.

Jay looked over at the grease cooking on the stove, then looked at his brother, cracked a smile, and shook his head.

"I was only trying to help," Von said and walked out as Nivea started preparing the chicken to fry.

Von went back and sat on the coach next to Tammy. He wrapped his arm around her and began to whisper in her ear about how he couldn't wait to bend her over.

୧୨୫୬

This lying son of a bitch, Coco thought when saw Von's truck parked in front of Jay's house. She parked her truck on the other side of the street and cut it off. She sat there thinking about what she would do if Von was in there with another bitch. He had to be. Why in the hell else didn't he want her to come? And to hell with the lame-ass shit about her and Nivea not liking each other! No, they didn't like each other, but there were plenty of times that they had put up with each other for the sake of Von and Jay—like the time when she had come over to see the baby when he was born.

"He is so full of shit. I am getting so sick of his ass."

Tears began to run down her face. Von hadn't treated Coco as though he wanted her in a long time. She often thought that he was only with her because of the baby. If that was the case, he would have to tell her straight up, because she wasn't going anywhere. Like Beyonce said, "Ring the muthafuckin alarm." She'd be damned if she would see another bitch on his arms. She'd put up with too much shit to just sit back and let him go make the next bitch happy. It wasn't happening.

Coco took off her coat and stepped out of the car. It was still drizzling, so she placed the coat over her head and hurried across the street. Once she was on the porch, she put her jacket back on and rang the doorbell. Thinking about what she was about to see on the other side of the door, her heart rate began to increase and her nose flared.

When the door opened, she bit her bottom lip. "Hey, Jay, I came to watch the fight."

Jay had already seen Coco through the peephole and warned his brother that she was there. Von, being the man that he was, told Tammy that his crazy baby-momma was at the door, and to fall back and act as if they weren't together.

When Coco walked in the house, she took in everyone and everything going on. Seeing Von sitting alone, she calmed down just a bit; but the way that the girl with the jet-black hair was looking at her, she assumed that she had beef, and Von was the reason.

"Which one of these bitches are you talking to, Von?" She pointed to Tammy. "I think it's that bitch right there because she keeps staring like she has a problem."

"Here we go," he mumbled. Tammy laughed.

"Bitch, what's funny? You see something funny?" She walked over to her. "As a matter of fact, who are you?" Coco was now all up in her face.

"Jay, what is going on?"

Nivea had heard the commotion and come out of the kitchen. She looked over at Coco and shook her head. This was her first time seeing her guests since they had arrived. She watched as Coco stood in front of the girl, and Von was trying to pull her away. She automatically knew he and his baby-momma were the cause of the drama.

"Come, sit down; she's here with Boo," he lied as he pulled her over to the other couch.

Jay tried taking the attention off Von and Coco by putting Nivea in the spotlight. "Did you guys speak to my wife?"

"Hey," they all said in unison.

Nivea didn't bother speaking back. She turned to walk back to the kitchen. "You smell that?" She looked at Jay, and right before he went to answer, the smoke detector began to scream, followed behind a cloud of smoke coming out of the kitchen."Oh my God, my chicken," Nivea yelled. Then she covered up her mouth and started for the kitchen.

"Open the doors and go outside." Jay said to his guests and ran toward the kitchen; Von followed him.

CR80

The house was too smoky to go back inside, so Nivea and the guests stood on the porch, waiting for the smoke to clear out. It wasn't as bad as it seemed, but the chicken had burned up. As Jay and Von were coming out of the house, Nivea was walking in.

"Where are you going?" Jay questioned.

"To the restroom," she said, never looking back. She was embarrassed and disappointed at herself for messing up dinner. Then she thought, *It's Coco and Von's fault. If they hadn't come over with that ghetto madness, then she would have still been in the kitchen, attending to her food.*

Von looked at Nivea as she hurried into the house and laughed. Coco noticed what he was laughing at, and she, too, started laughing.

"I'm about to hit Wing Stop," Jay told his guests.

54

"You should have done that in the first place," Von said, adding in his two cents.

His brother turned and looked at him. That's when he noticed the red 2013 Aston Martin Rapide sitting in front of the house.

"Whose shit is that?" Jay asked, looking at his brother.

"Nigga, it ain't yours." Von joked.

"You only got that car because you know I wanted one." Jay walked off the porch and headed to the car.

"No, I didn't, but look . . ." Von said as he followed Jay over to the car. He couldn't wait to show it off.

Travis had gone back into the house to make sure everything was good. It was, so he told the others to come back inside. Jay and Von cooed a little longer, until Jay took his brother's keys to go to Wing Stop. He couldn't wait to drive that bad boy.

ᘓᘔ

Jay wanted to play around in the car so he decided to hit Wing Stop way on the other side of town. As he drove down Crenshaw, he was spotted by some niggas in a blue, old-school Chevy Impala.

"There's that nigga Von right there, the driver told the passenger.

"That nigga must be stupid coming on this side of town. He really must think he owns L.A."

The driver of the Impala busted a U-turn in the middle of the street and tailed who they thought was Von. When Jay pulled into the little shopping center, the driver parked by Wienerschnitzel and watched as Jay got out of the Aston and walked into Wing Stop.

"Call the homies and let them know that that bitch-ass nigga is in the hood."

"I'm on it," said the passenger as he placed the phone to his ear and waited for an answer.

Von was well-known all over the county. While most knew that he had an identical twin, there were still a few who didn't, and the niggas who wanted his head were part of that few. Von hadn't done anything to them personally, but a few weeks back, after a dispute over who had been the first one to bang the Latin hottie who worked at McDonald's, Von had ended up pistol whipping their big homie. Von wasn't trying to take it there—the shit was petty to him—but the fool wouldn't let it go. He went all big and shit, calling Von out of his name. That was a straight no-no. Unknown to Von, it really wasn't about the bitch who worked at McDonald's. The nigga didn't like him simply because Von's money was longer than his, and Von had the bitch he wanted. After he'd pistol-whipped him, the shit had gotten real and that nigga Von was about to pay.

"He's inside Wing Stop, right here on the Shaw. Y'all come up here. We ain't strapped," the passenger informed the person on the other end of the phone. "Nigga, we're on the way," the person on the other end assured him. Then he hung up the phone and looked at the goons sitting in the house with him. "Let's roll. That nigga Von is in our hood." They got up, grabbed their guns off the coffee table, and headed out of the door.

CRSD

JayVon was inside Wing Stop, standing on the side of the counter waiting on his order, when he noticed two dudes enter mean-mugging him. He was wondering what was up with that; he'd never seen the fools before. On top of that, he had no beef with anybody. It never dawned on him that they could have mistaken him for his twin brother. Being JayVon, he shrugged it off and began to mess around with his cell phone. About five minutes later, after the dudes had walked out, his order was called. JayVon put his cell in his pocket, grabbed his order, and walked out of the restaurant.

"Fuck-ass nigga, you must really think you are untouchable?" Jay heard someone say. That's when he looked up and saw two of the dudes who had just mean-mugged him, sitting in a Chevy Impala, staring at him.

"What?" Jay asked, walking towards the driver's side of his brother's Ashton.

"Nigga, fuck you!" said another dude who he hadn't seen. He was standing on the side of a blue van with his hands in his pants. JayVon shook his head and continued toward his vehicle.

"So you acting like a bitch now that your homeboys ain't with you?" the dude said who was standing by the van.

"Look, nigga, I don't know you and you don't know me. Chill with that shit." JayVon sat the box of chicken in the car and went to get in when shots were fired.

The first bullet caught him the stomach. "Arrrrggggghhhh . . ." He hunched over in pain. The burning sensation was excruciating. Boc. Boc. Another hit him in his shoulder. "Fuck," Jay mumbled. *These niggas is straight going to kill me,* he thought just before the last bullet hit him in the collarbone, dropping him to the ground.

Even after Jay was down, all three of the shooters continued to empty their guns. People were screaming and ducking for cover.

"Let's go, big homey," the dude in the Impala hollered at their homeboy who was empting the remainder of his clip into

JayVon's car. It wasn't until he had no more bullets that he jumped in his van and fled the scene. He was sure that the nigga was dead.

CRSO

Brandy

Tears filled Brandy's eyes as she rode down the highway, weaving in and out of traffic. The rain had just slacked up, and she wanted badly to let down her window to feel the breeze—that would have helped relax her mind—but it was still sprinkling, and she didn't want the inside of her car or her hair to get wet, so letting down the windows was a no-no.

She shook her head at the thought of this evening's events. She couldn't understand where she'd gone wrong. In fact, she never did; but that was her life living with Robert Hicks. A good, relaxing day was what she'd wanted but, as usual, she never got what she wanted.

To get her mind off what had gone down at her place, she thought it would be a good idea to chill with Coco; maybe go to a sports bar and have a few drinks while watching the fight. But, as always, Coco and the infamous Von had plans. Brandy rolled her eyes when she thought about how good Coco had it. She had a man who made her happy and loved her and, per Coco, the sex was A-1. When Coco talked about her man, Brandy would feel salty because she wanted what Coco had. Why couldn't she have what Coco had? She was a good person.

"Lord, when will I get the love and security that I deserve?" Brandy spoke aloud.

More tears ran down her face as she pulled up to a stop sign and thought about what had just happened between her and the nigga Rob she was cursed with.

CRSO

Damn, didn't I just call him? The least he could have done was open the door, knowing I was going to be carrying these heavy-ass bags, *Brandy thought as she balanced a brown-paper grocery bag in each arms, and a bottle of Hennessy in her hand, which was his request for her to bring back. To be honest, she really hated when he drank liquor because he didn't know how to control his hands. He would often beat the hell out of her if she said or did things he didn't "approve" of. The one thing she did enjoy was the makeup sex after she was no longer angry with him. He wasn't the best she'd ever had, but he was sometimes good at what he did, especially with his mouth; plus, the sex made her feel wanted and loved.*

Walking up the stairs that led to her two-bedroom condo, she could hear the loud music coming from her unit. The closer she got to the door, the stronger the smell of the marijuana.

"I know damn well he is not smoking in the house and my baby's in there," she said, marching up to the door faster. He knows these neighbors are nosy as hell."

She shook her head at his foolishness. Brandy was so pissed off by the mere fact of being with him. She'd told herself countless times that things would change . . . if only she knew when.

When Brandy made it to her door, she turned around backwards and used the back of her foot to kick the door. She did it a couple of times before she realized that he wouldn't be able to hear her over the loud music. She set the bags down on the porch, then shuffled around in her purse for the house keys.

This is one ignorant nigga, she thought as she opened the door and the stench of smoke smacked her in the face. She was beyond pissed when she saw the same old lame-ass niggas in her house. No one offered to help her with the bags; they just sat on her couch enjoying her electricity.

Brandy set the bags on the floor by the door and speed-walked past them to her son's room. She eased the door open and peeked in the room. Her baby, sleeping peacefully, put a smile on her face. Her smile vanished when she turned to go back in the living room. She was going to give Rob a piece of her mind

"Heyyyy, babyyyy . . ." Rob's words were slurred; he was tipsy from the few beers he had drank. He stood from the couch and turned to his boys. "Yo, we're about to eat good, and get fucked up now." He looked at Brandy. "My baby is here. Bae, where's the Henn? Did you forget what I told you to bring?"

Brandy knew that Rob hated an out-of-line woman more than he hated to be fronted, but that was his problem. She was pissed off, and he and his friends were going to know it. She looked at his friends and rolled her eyes. Then she looked at Rob.

"I need to see you in the kitchen. Now, please." She turned and walked off.

"Did this bitch . . ." Rob mumbled as he looked at his boys. "Y'all give me a min— Let me go holla at her." He started to follow Brandy in the kitchen, but noticed his brother and his friends get up. "What's up?" he asked.

They all knew what was about to go down, and they wanted to get out of there before it happened. None of them wanted to be involved or be a witness to a domestic-violence tragedy. The last time, he'd beaten her until she looked like the elephant woman. They'd almost had to jump on him to get him off her, only to turn around and she was back with him. They were out of it. As Rob's mother had said, "When she wants out, she'll get out—if he doesn't kill her first."

"We'll catch up with you later, man," his lil brother said, and they all headed toward the door.

"Man, why y'all leaving? We've still got plenty to drink and the fight don't start for another hour"

"Just hit us later," one of the boys hollered over his shoulder as he closed the door behind him.

Rob was now even more upset, "I'm going to teach this bitch some manners," he huffed and headed for the kitchen. "Fucking fat bitch," he added.

After Brandy had had the baby, she'd picked up twenty pounds. Standing at an even five foot, nine inches, and weighing one hundred ninety pounds, with big boobs and a plum bottom, Rob swore she was the most disgusting woman walking. If one were to put her picture next to Jill Scott, and add a short bob cut, you would swear they were sisters. Brandy never had a problem with self-esteem issues until after she gave birth to her and Rob's baby. Now, she was always dieting, but it never lasted because of him. He stressed her, which caused her to eat.

Brandy was standing at the kitchen counter with her back turned. She had a glass of water in her hand, lifting it to her mouth to take a drink when, out of nowhere, her head jerked back and the glass fell out of her hand. Rob had yanked her hair so hard that it felt like her hair was being detached from her scalp. Brandy fell back on the floor, one hand holding her head and the other wrapped around his wrist.

"Come on, you dumb bitch. It's time to put you back through training."

He began to drag her from the kitchen. She was whimpering, but Rob didn't give a damn if he'd yanked her head off. He kept his tight grip until he dragged her back where it all started, the living room.

"Stop please, Rob. Ouch!" Brandy tried taking his hand from her hair; but it was no use, he was too strong. "Why are you acting like this? All I wanted to do was talk to you," she cried.

Once they were back in the living room, he let her hair go. Breathing heavily, he hovered over Brandy,

"Stand up," he demanded, and she did. "Now I want you to take that fat, nasty ass of yours back out that door," he pointed his finger toward the front door, "and bring your ass back in here and greet me like the king I am."

Hearing the words coming from Rob's mouth made her feel small and stupid; but to prevent an ass whipping, she did as she was told. Rob watched as she walked out of the door.

"Lord, help me, please. Why do I still love him?" she silently prayed as she reentered the living room.

"Hey, baby, how was your day?"

She walked up to him and mustered up the best smile she could. She perched her lips to kiss him as she went to hug him at the same time, and . . . SMACK! He backhanded her so hard that she fell back on the couch and blood poured from her nose. "Ahhhh noooo!" she screamed, holding her nose, but Rob wasn't done with her yet. Brandy jumped from the couch and tried to run, but he caught her by the neck and slammed her onto the floor, causing a loud thump sound.

"Where do you think you're going, bitch, huh? You're too big to outrun me." He kicked her in the leg. "Any other time when I tell your fat ass to run, you sit your fat, lazy ass around here and stuff your fucking face, but now you want to run?" he said all in one breath, then began to repeatedly hit her on her arms, legs, and stomach—all areas that she could cover up with makeup or clothing. He knew she needed to go to work, so he wasn't trying to mess up her face.

The entire time Brandy stayed balled up in a fetal position. After five minutes of delivering blow after blow and kick after kick, Rob was tired and out of breath. He figured she'd learned her lesson, so he didn't attempt to try to get enough energy to hit her again.

"Get up and fix me a drink," he huffed. He turned and walked over to the couch, where he flopped down and kicked his feet up on the stool.

Brandy lay there, crying her heart out; it just wasn't fair that she had to suffer as she did. She was good to the broke-ass nigga, and beatings were how he repaid her?

"Get up, bitch, before I get back over there and beat your ass again," he growled. Hearing cries come from the back room, he got up to check on his son. He knew for sure the bitch would have his drink when he came back; he didn't even bother to tell her again.

CRSO

HONK. HONK. HONK. The driver behind Brandy blew at her several times before she was pulled from her trance. Brandy pulled off and turned into the Starbuck's parking lot, two driveways down. She needed something hot to help relax her, and a few minutes to clear her mind. As she sat in the Starbuck's drive-thru, she couldn't get Rob off her mind. She shook her head as she thought, *Enough is enough!* She was fed-up with him. He wasn't only physically and mentally abusive, but he was the lazy, pot-bellied fuck that he claimed she was.

Everything he'd promised her was a lie, and every word that came out his pitiful mouth was negative. He was never supportive of her dreams. The entire time she had gone to school to become an RN, he'd said that she wouldn't make it; but as soon as she graduated and was hired by the County of Los Angeles, he was all for spending her money. "Ugh!" she screamed. Why in the hell she was in love with a deadbeat, she didn't know. She told herself that if she had taken heed to the signs in the beginning, she wouldn't be in this situation.

CRƎࡍ

Brandy had met Rob at a house party. She would never forget how he'd flossed, acting as if the all-white, 2011 Lexus was his; come to find out, it was his homeboy's ride. That night, he was looking real good to the eye—the brown-skinned, bald head, six-foot-one brother was well-built and had swag that was all that and then some. All she could think about when he'd stepped to her was how she snagged a nigga who looked good and had money.

The first night they'd met, she was thinking about him blowing her back out. They didn't have sex that same night, but they did a few weeks later. And she'd ended up pregnant. Shortly after that, she'd found out that he was nothing but a fake. Not only was the car that he driving not his, but the fool was broke. He'd recently been released from jail, and lived at home with his mother and brother. His clothes were hand-me-downs from his boys because he'd lost all his clothes when he'd done his five-year bid. Brandy was too through when she asked him one day about his gold grill; he'd had one when they met and the few times they'd hooked up. Come to find out, the shits were pullouts.

Instead of calling him out on what he was—a worthless piece of shit—she made him her own. She didn't believe in abortion, and she didn't want her baby growing up as she had, in a single-parent home. She'd decided to make it work. Rob had lied for months about different jobs he had lined up, and how he was going to come up with money to help pay her bills; it had never happened. Eventually he had stopped lying, and when she asked him about it, he would snap or ask her what she was doing with her money.

CRSO

"Welcome to Starbuck's. How can I help you?" the voice from the intercom boomed with enthusiasm.

"Hmmmm . . . Let me have a tall vanilla latte."

The Starbuck's employee thanked her for her order and asked her to pull forward.

CB&O

Back at JayVon & Nivea's

The title fight had finally come on, and everyone was all into it. The grand, ghetto-fabulous entry Coco had made and Nivea's burning up the chicken were things of the past. Mayweather and his opponent were now in their third round, and the heat was beginning to turn up.

"Yeah, homie, it's about to be a done deal this round," one of the brothers said to one of the others, and they gave each other dap.

"Naw, son, Mayweather's gotta step his game up if he thinks he's about to get another win in. Alvarez ain't playing with that boy," said Travis He looked over at Von, who was sitting in the corner watching quietly. That was unlike him.

"Wake up, nigga, you sleep ova there?" Travis teased.

"Shut up, nigga, and put your money up," Von shot back, trying to act as if he was back in tune with the fight, but he wasn't. Something wasn't right. He could feel it deep down within.

Trying to block the alien feeling in his gut, Von continued to try to focus on the jabs Mayweather was giving his opponent. "Damn," he mumbled. It was as if every time Mayweather hit his opponent, Von could feel it. Mayweather gave a right jab to Alvarez' midsection, then a few quick hits to his ribcage. "Humn." He doubled over and put his hands across his chest.

Coco, never the one to miss a beat when it came to her man, questioned, "What's the matter, baby? Are you alright? You didn't eat anything here did you?"

Von didn't answer her. He was too busy trying to figure out what in the hell was going on. He only got that feeling when something was wrong with those who were close to him, and the emotions were so strong, there had to be something going on with his brother.

CR80

He and his brother were split up when they were eight. Von moved down to L.A. with his father, and Jay stayed in Palmdale with his grandmother. One day Jay was outside playing, fell off his bike, and broke his arm. Far away in another city, Von had felt a sharp pain in the same arm, and had barely been able to move it for hours. Later that night, he found out that it was the same arm his brother had broken. As the years went by, they found out it was a connection that twins have; that was the first of many.

CʒꙄꙄ

What the fuck is wrong with my brother? Still holding his chest with one hand, he reached for his cell with the other.

"Von, baby, are you ready to leave?" Coco asked with a concerned look on her face.

Von started to respond when his cell phone rang. It was one of his workers in L.A. "S'up, Itty Bitty?" he answered the phone.

"Nigga, damn, you don't know how good it feels to hear your voice. Man, I just saw a car like yours surrounded by yellow tape. The nigga that was hit was shot like twelve times; the car looks like Swiss cheese."

"That's my brother!" he shouted. "Where you at?"

When dude told him he was by Wing Stop on Crenshaw, it confirmed what he already knew.

"Awww, hell naw!" Itty Bitty took off running across the street. "Let me go see where they're taking him. They are putting him in the truck now."

Von hung up the phone. "TRAV, LET'S GO!" Von's alarmed tone alerted the others. They watched as he jumped up from the stool, almost knocking Coco over, and touched his waist.

"What's up, fam?" asked Travis as he touched his waist where his gun was.

Von could barely get the words out. After swallowing the lump that formed in his throat, he replied, "Jay's been shot!"

Von was hit with a barrage of questions, but he didn't bother to answer any of them. He looked at Coco, who was standing with her hand covering her mouth. "I need to call my nigga Itty Bitty back and find out where they took him." He stopped talking and took a deep breath. He put his hand on his chest and slowly let out his breath, then things went black.

Coco touched him. "Baby . . . Von . . . Are you alright?"

Her touch and voice brought him back. He looked at her. "Get Niv to the hospital. Tell her Jay has been shot."

Although Coco wouldn't be a good person to break the news to her, since they didn't see eye-to-eye, there wasn't any other choice. "Okay, baby." She watched as her man and his crew ran out of the door.

CRSO

Nivea really didn't want to entertain anyone, especially not the ride-or-die-for-their-thuggish-hoodlum-men females who were in her home. She really couldn't stand the sight of Coco, with her long, fake eyelashes, blonde hair, and the hoochie attire that she always seemed to wear. To Niv, everything about her screamed, "Gold digger and ratchet." Neither Coco nor the others were the type of females she would ever hang around, and that's why she'd kept her distance by staying in the kitchen.

While Jay was gone to get the hot wings, she thought of the idea of feeding the unwanted guests Patron shots in hopes of them getting drunk so they would leave to go bone the girls, or to do whatever it was that they did. As she filled each of the eight shot glasses with Tequila, she wondered what was taking Jay so long. *I'll call him after I serve these people*; she thought as she picked up the tray and walked out of the kitchen. Careful not to spill the shots, Nivea slowly walked down the hall. As she was turning the corner into the family room, she stopped in her tracks and gasped.

"Take Nivea to the hospital. Jay has been shot."

She got an instant migraine. Her breathing began to speed up, and she got weak, causing her to drop the tray she was holding. Glass and liquor flew everywhere.

"Oh my . . . Oh my . . ."

She held her chest and leaned back on the wall. She felt as if she was going to pass out, but she couldn't do that. Jay . . . Her husband needed her. "I have to get to my husband," she managed to say as she sprung from the wall and ran into the living room.

Coco, hearing the glass break, looked in the hallway. Upon seeing Nivea's state, and thinking about how she would have acted if it were Von who had gotten hurt, Coco's heart softened just a bit and she ran after her.

"Nivea, hold up. I need to call Von to see what hospital they took him to," she yelled behind her.

Coco then looked at the two girls who were still there. She put on a mean-mug, and demanded that they get the hell out of there. They wasted no time grabbing their things and leaving. As Coco was locking the door behind them, she could hear the engine roar from Nivea's Rover. She grabbed her purse off the couch and took off running out of the side door that led to the garage.

"Nivea, get out and let me drive. Von is on the line." She held up the phone. "They took him to Big General. Come on, let me drive you."

Nivea stared into space as she slid out of the driver's seat and over to the passenger seat. Coco jumped in the truck and burned rubber all the way to the hospital. While Nivea was hoping that Jay was alright and wondering what could have happened, Coco was thanking God that it wasn't Von who was hurt. She wouldn't have been able to handle it.

Chapter Three

Jay

JayVon lay in the back of the EMT truck on a gurney, trying his best to stay alert; but the gunshot wounds to his chest, back, and leg were making it very hard

"Stay with us, son, and fight," he heard a man say as he applied pressure on his chest, causing his body to jerk up and then back down.

"Man, it burns; I think I'm about to pass out," he replied, but no one heard him. The words never left his mouth.

"I think we're losing him. Come on, stay with us."

"I'm trying, but the pain is making it hard. Did someone call my brother? What about my wife? Tell them I love them."

JayVon began to lose conscious. As much as he wanted to fight, the pain was making it too hard. "Nivea, Nivea Deeds is my wife," was the last thing he tried to tell the worker before he faded out. Tears seeped from his closed eyelids and ran down the side of his face. Knowing that he would never be able to be with his wife or brother again was starting to hurt more than the gunshot wounds.

"Baby, don't cry. Dry your eyes." JayVon's heart fluttered when he heard the sound of his mother's voice. He hadn't heard her sweet voice since she had been murdered. That had been over twenty years ago; but it was as comforting to him now as it had been when he was a child and she'd said those words to him. He knew that she would take care of him. "Grandma and I miss you so much," the voice continued. He wanted to speak back to her, but he was scared that it was a dream, and she would disappear. Suddenly, a light brighter than the sun appeared over him. Wearing all white and sharing the same pretty smile were the first two women he'd ever given his heart. First, his mother, then his grandmother, held their arms out and assured him, "You are safe with us. No more pain."

CR80

Von

In the waiting room, Von paced back and forth. The entire hour that they had been there, he hadn't had a seat. All kinds of questions bombarded his mind: *Who did it? How had it happened? Why had it happened? Will he survive? What if he dies? On my dead daddy, I am going to merc the niggas who did this. Naw, they will die a slow death.*

Von began to breathe heavily. The more he thought, the angrier he became. "Fuckkkk!" he yelled; then he punched the wall, causing the drywall to cave in. He placed his head against the wall. "This shit is all my fault. I should have gone to get the wings. I should have gone with him. Man, that should be me." He held in his tears. In his heart, he knew his brother was gone, and maybe he was in a better place, but he couldn't handle it.

"It's my job to look after my baby bro, man," he said, finally breaking down.

Travis looked over at his cousin, and his heart was heavy. He knew how much they loved each other. Jay was a cool guy who tried to do right by his life, and Von had always admired that. So to know that he was the cause of his brother being hurt, he knew that was eating him up inside. He also knew that L.A. County would never be the same.

Travis walked over to where Von was and placed his hand on his back. "It's going to be alright, man. Be strong. I'm going to find the niggas who did this, even if it takes my last breath." Travis didn't wait for Von to respond. He walked outside. He needed some air.

Coco was rubbing Von's back. "Baby, he's a fighter. You know that; both of you are tough. You know, just like the rest of us, that Jay isn't going out like that. We all know that he likes a good challenge." Coco wrapped her arms around him, and laid her head on his back. "He's going to pull through. I'm here for you, baby. I ain't going anywhere," she assured him. Von may have been a cheating dog, but she loved him and his money, and she wasn't going anywhere.

Nivea was sitting in the corner, away from everyone, with her knees pulled into her chest, rocking back and forth. "Please, God, let him be o.k. Please God, don't take my baby." She had been praying the same prayer nonstop. She was trying her best not to lose her mind, but she had no control over her cool. Hearing Von blame himself, and Coco telling him that everything would be o.k., was pushing her closer to the edge. *He's damn right; it was his fault. And how in the hell did Coco know if her husband would pull through? She wasn't a fucking doctor,* she thought as she rocked faster.

She was beginning to see red. What put the icing on the cake was when Travis said, he was "going to get the people back who were responsible for shooting her husband." *This must have something to do with them and the lifestyle they live,* her inner voice said. Then Coco said, "Baby, come sit down. Come on. Do you need some water?"

That did it; it was too much for her. Being in the room with the people who could possibly be responsible for her husband's condition, waiting on the doctor to deliver some kind of news, and Coco acting as if Von was the victim, had her thirty-eight hot.

Nivea hopped up from the chair "YOU'RE DAMN RIGHT IT'S YOUR FAULT." She pointed her finger toward Von. "YOU OUGHT TO BE ASHAMED OF YOURSELF. YOU ARE BLOOD, HIS TWIN, AND YOU ARE THE CAUSE OF ALL OF THIS. HE HATES THE LIFE YOU LIVE. HE ASKED YOU TO GET OUT THE GAME, MANY TIMES, BEFORE SOMETHING HAPPENED, AND YOU NEVER LISTENED. NOW LOOK WHAT YOU'VE DONE. LOOK WHAT YOU'VE CAUSED!" she cried. She was hurting and angry. "It should be your sorry ass in that bed fighting for your life, not my precious husband." She looked at everyone in the room. "You are all a pathetic waste of life and I hope—"

Cutting her off in mid-sentence, Coco twirled her neck and went off. "Bitch, you must be smoking something. Who in the hell are you calling a pathetic waste?" She put her hands on her hips, and looked Nivea up and down. "You ain't shit. Ya daddy ain't shit. Your mamma had to run off and trick with a black nigga just so you could look halfway decent, you ugly hoe." Coco had been waiting for the day that she could serve Nivea's stuck-up ass, and she'd finally gotten it. "And if wasn't for all that plastic surgery, your ass and breasts would be flat just like your rice-eating grandma's. Don't think for one second that you're all that because you're a half breed; you're still an ugly hoe." Coco rolled up her sleeves. "You know what? Fuck all this talking." Coco began taking her bamboo earrings out of her ear. She was about to tap that ass.

"Sit your ass down, Co," Von warned, never taking his eyes off Nivea. He wanted to slap the shit out of Nivea for talking shit, but it wasn't the time or place, and Coco should have had enough sense to know that.

"Naw, scratch that mess you're talking, Von. I've been waiting for the day when this bitch would jump bad, so that I could give her this ghetto-fab ass whipping she's been asking for. Bring it, Miss Classy," Coco said, all hyped up and taking a step to lunge at her.

In one with swift motion, Von grabbed Coco around the neck and applied a little pressure to his grip. He whispered, "I told you to sit your stupid ass down. This is neither the day nor the place. Do I make myself clear?" he squeezed a little tighter.

With tears rolling down her face, she nodded her head yes. He let her neck go and pushed her down in the chair with a mean glare, then demanded that she go home. Without looking at anyone, Coco got up from the chair and grabbed her bag sitting on a chair across the room. She didn't even bother to mention the fact that her car was still at Nivea and Jay's. She just wanted to get the hell out of there. She was so hurt and embarrassed.

As Coco was walking out, a nurse was coming in; she didn't bother to hear the news that she was about to deliver. She simply hurried out of the waiting room and called her sidekick Dre. *Fuck Von,* she thought as she whipped the tears flowing from her eyes.

"If you guys do not cut out all that noise, I will have security escort you out. There are other families going through things as well. You are too loud and disrespectful," said the nurse who entered the waiting room.

An angry Von looked around the waiting room. "Everyone get the fuck out. Now!" Von demanded. One by one everyone left the room including the nurse. It was now only him and Nivea there. If looks could knock you upside the head, kick you around the room, then kill you, Nivea would be one beat up, dead woman.

The way Von was staring at Nivea had her scared shitless, but she wasn't about to let him know. If she had to fight him tooth-and-nail, she wasn't about to back down. After all, it *was* his fault. Nivea cleared her throat and stood tall. "I meant every word I said." She rolled her eyes and took a seat.

Von wanted nothing more than to let Coco tap that ass, but it wasn't the right place or the right time. That shit she had been talking, he'd written off as her not being able to deal with what was going on. He knew what she was saying was how she really felt but, at the moment, it was fuck her feelings and all about his brother.

୧୫୭

The Phone Call

"What's up, Dre?" said the caller when Dre answered the phone; his tone was aggravated and disgusted.

"Nigga, you tell me," Dre responded.

"What's up is you touched the wrong nigga. Why in the fuck didn't you get at me before you gave your boys the go?" The caller was furious. Since Dre had touched the wrong person and let the right one live, he had just started a war that neither was ready for.

"First of all, I handled the shit myself. That's what gangsters do. That's to prove I'm a real nigga and to make sure the job was done properly. Second of all, nigga, don't call my phone coming at me like I'm some punk. That's the reason *that* nigga got touched in

84

the first place. Now do your part so we can get paid and go our separate ways," Dre retorted.

"Nigga, I can't do shit now. It's out of my hands. That was his twin brother who was shot." The caller shook his head in aversion. Shit was already going wrong.

"His twin? Fuck outta here. Look, homey, don't try to play me." Dre's temples began to throb.

"That. Was. His. Fucking. TWIN!" the caller reiterated before hanging up on Dre.

"Hello? Hello?" Dre looked at his phone. "This nigga hung up on me." Dre was pissed, but he would deal with it later. Dre thought about how he could confirm that the nigga was telling the truth. He and the caller had been in cahoots for a few months, and the nigga had never mentioned that Von's punk ass had a twin. *That nigga is probably lying,* he thought.

Then it hit him. *She'll know. All I gotta do is tell her that I heard what happened and wanted to see if she was alright.* Just as Dre went through his Contacts list on his phone to look for her number, she was calling. "Baby girl, I was just thinking about you. Are you alright?"

CRSO

Later . . .

An hour had gone by, and Von and Nivea were still waiting to hear the outcome of Jay's condition. They both were worried out of their minds and needed the other, but their stubbornness and pride wouldn't allow them to come together. Every minute that went by, they became more intense; but on the flipside, it gave them more hope. It could only mean that Jay was fighting for his life.

As Von sat thinking about how he was going to cut the niggas heads off who had brought this to his brother, Nivea prayed that she would be able to lie in his arms again. Finally, an older man with salt-and-pepper hair and a white coat walked in, and introduced himself as Dr. Ramon, the surgeon. Nivea and Von hopped up at the same time. Looking at Von, the doctor did a double take.

"I'm Von, his brother, and that's his wife, Nivea." Von cut his eyes at her.

"Son, if I didn't know any better, I would have thought you just followed me out of the surgery room." The doctor chuckled to lighten the mood.

"I often hear that there is someone out there who looks just like me." Von joked back, but his tone was dry.

Nivea had no time for the foolishness they were talking. "How is my husband?"

"Take a seat," the doctor requested.

"No," Nivea and Von replied.

"Fair enough." Dr. Ramon, looking Nivea in the eye, said, "Your husband was shot three times. We were able to take out the bullet that was in his leg; but the ones in his chest and back, we don't want to remove because we fear we might lose him. Both bullets are close to his main artery. He is very lucky to still be alive, although there is still a slight chance that he may not make it." He then looked at Von. "Your brother is in a coma."

"A coma? He may not make it? Oh my God, no!" Nivea felt her breathing accelerate. Feeling as if her legs would give out on her at anytime, she grabbed hold of Von's arm.

"I need to see my brother." Von's voice cracked.

"Give us a few hours to get him settled in ICU, and someone will come out to escort you over. Like I said, he is in a coma, so he won't know you are there."

Nivea broke down crying. Von wanted to break down as well, but he knew he had to stay strong. He held her and allowed her to cry on his chest.

Coco

"What, dang? Why are you looking at me like that?" Coco frowned up her face as she looked at Dre. She had called Dre to pick her up from the hospital and take her back to Nivea and Jay's to get her truck. She'd started to go pick up her baby and go home, but all she would have done there was cry her eyes out.

Her feelings was really hurt, and she wanted Dre to help make her feel better; but he was getting on her nerves with all the questions about the shooting and the daggers he was shooting because Von hadn't made sure she'd gotten to her car safely. If she had told him how Von had treated her at the hospital in front of everyone, he would have really had some shit to say. That's why she'd kept her mouth closed.

Dre hated that nigga Von, and never could understand what Von had that he didn't. Coco used her and Von's child as the reason she stayed, but the truth of the matter was she really loved him. Plus, Von's money was longer than Dre's, but she wouldn't tell him that.

"What do you mean, why am I looking at you like that? Because your ass only comes around me when you're in a bad mood. You could have taken that shit home. I ain't trying to be fucked with on no rebound type of shit."

Nigga, that's all it's been, a rebound relationship, thought Coco as she and Dre stared eye-to-eye.

"A nigga ain't ugly. I could have three or four bitches, but I chose you." Dre pointed at her. He wasn't lying. Dre was very handsome. He wasn't that tall, maybe five-nine, and two hundred twenty pounds of muscle. He was a light-skinned dude, rocking a bald head, with light brown eyes, and freckles on his nose. He wasn't packing, but he could put it down in the bedroom, and he had money. The females stayed on him.

Back in high school when he and Coco had first hooked up, she was constantly fighting over him. It wasn't until he was locked up that she had moved on and hooked up with Von. Thirteen months later, when Dre got out, she had given birth to her son, and Dre was cool on her. The two had just started back kicking it about six months ago. That was when Coco had found out about the little bitch from the east side who Von was messing with.

CR80

After putting the baby to sleep, Coco and Von decided to watch a movie together. The two of them were sitting on the couch, chilling, when Coco got a text that said, 'Watch this video,' and

there was a link for her to click. Immediately Coco thought it was
*spam, so she paid it no mind, but she did text back to say, '*Stop
texting my shit you hacker.*' A few seconds later, she got another*
*text that said, '*Bitch, click the video and find out the real about
that nigga Von.*'*

Coco looked up at Von, who was all into the movie they were
watching. She thought about telling him about the message, but
changed her mind. She wanted to see it first, so she got up and
walked to the bedroom. Once in the bedroom, Coco's hands began
to shake and her heart was racing faster than a nigga's trying to
outrun the police. She could only imagine what was on the video.
When she finally clicked on the video, she saw Von with some
chick who looked like she was about nineteen or twenty giving him
a lap dance that turned into a blowjob, and him fucking her from
the back, bareback. She broke down crying.

"You sorry son-of-a-bitch, I hate you," she screamed as she
stood in front of Von with the cell phone in her hand.

Von looked up at her. He knew her distraught attitude was
about something she had found out, and nine times out of ten, it
was true; but he would never admit to it. "Man, stop all that
yelling and shit; the baby is sleep. What's the problem?"

Coco threw the phone at him and it hit him in the chest. He snatched the phone from his lap and hurled it at the wall, causing it to break. "What did I tell you about putting your hands on me?" He jumped up.

"Ain't anybody put their hands on you, but you put your hands and raw dick all in the next bitch." She stood face-to-face with him. "Really, Von, not only are you cheating, but you're hitting bitches RAW, a stripper bitch at that?"

How in the fuck did she see that? I wonder if she's talking about the afterhours, *thought Von.*

Coco walked over to where her phone was lying on the floor and picked it up. When saw that the screen was shattered, she chuckled. "Nigga, you know what you were doing by breaking my phone, but it's cool. You do you and I will do me."

Coco turned and walked out of the living room into her and Von's room. When she came out of the room, she was dressed in a mini-dress and high heels. She didn't even look at him when she walked out the door. She thought he would come after her, but he didn't.

That night, Coco ended up going to Spike's, a bar in Bellflower; that's where she saw Dre. The two chatted and she told him all about what was going on in her life. Dre claimed he wasn't *a rebound-type of nigga, but he knew that was how he'd gotten her. He knew that giving her the love and attention that she wasn't getting from Von would keep her.*

CR&SO

"Look, Coco, I ain't trying to put you out or nothing, but I think you should go home. You've got a lot on your mind; you need sometime alone."

"Whatever, Dre." Coco stood up. She tried not to look at him because she didn't want him to see her eyes tearing up. She was extremely emotional; not one, but two, niggas had put her out in one day.

Dre watched as Coco reached for her bag, then fish around on the couch for her keys. When she looked up, he noticed the tears running down her face, and his heart got weak. He walked over to her and pulled her into his arms.

"Baby, stop crying. I'm here. I'm here if you'll let me all the way in." He held her tightly and Coco broke down. She was so tired of Von's shit. "Stop all that crying."

Dre grabbed her by the chin and made her look at him. The two stared into each other eyes for a few moments before Dre leaned in and gave her a kiss that made her putty in his hands. Dre was a damn good kisser; his kisses always made her weak. Without breaking their kiss, Dre picked Coco up and carried her to his room.

CRSO

Across Town at the Hospital . . .

The wait for the doctor to return to give them the okay to go seemed like a lifetime to Jay. Von had left out the room without saying a thing to Nivea. She wanted to ask him where he was going, but thought that maybe she should leave him be. Hopefully, he was going to rethink his lifestyle.

In the meantime, Nivea was lost in her thoughts. So many questions with no answers replayed repeatedly in Nivea's mind. She was worried sick. Out of all the years she and Jay had been together, she couldn't remember them ever being apart. Ever! Nivea never liked being at home alone. If Jay had a business meeting overnight, she would always go with him. Jay thought it was cute.

"Please fight, baby. I need you more now than ever," she softly whispered to herself thinking that, somehow, their spirits would connect, and he would hear her. She sure hoped so.

Nivea was staring at the floor when she saw a pair of J's appear in front of her; Von had returned. For that, she was secretly grateful. She was beginning to feel light-headed and weak. She laid her head back and shut her eyes for a few minutes to ease the headache that she knew only came from stress.

Von walked over and stood in front of Nivea, "I wasn't sure if you wanted coffee or water, so I got you both, and all they had was Tylenol."

A couple of seconds later, Nivea opened her eyes; slowly she raised her head from the back of the chair and looked up at Von. He was standing there holding a tray with two cups of coffee in it, a bottle of water, and the Tylenol in his other hand. *Hmmm, well, I guess he is good for something,* she thought as she sat up and took the cup of coffee, the water, and Tylenol from the tray. "Has it been two hours yet?"

"Almost, someone should be in here anytime now. If not, I will be out there grilling some damn body. I need to be near him," Von said, more to himself then to her.

"How did you know I like my coffee dark?" Nivea asked, shocked when she didn't see any creamers added in her cup.

"I didn't." He was nonchalant, not feeling how she hadn't even bothered to say 'thank you.' "I figured if you wanted extra then you would take your ass—" He didn't finish what he was about to say because Dr. Ramon came in, letting them know that they were able to go see JayVon.

The doctor led them down the hall, through two double doors. Passing up the nurses' station, they stopped at room 57B. Before stepping in the room, Nivea took deep, calming breaths. She was trying to calm her nerves before she walked in, but the technique didn't work. When she walked in and saw her Jay lying there with tubes down his nose and mouth, the big machine next to him making lots of noise, the bag with fluids running into a needle in his arm, it was a sight to see. It was too overwhelming for her. She placed her hand on her chest and a stream of crocodile tears ran down her face onto her blouse.

She put her hands over her mouth. "Oh my, baby, no!" Her shoulders began to shake uncontrollably. She couldn't stop crying.

Von stood on the left side of Nivea. Staring at his twin in that state, fucked with his heart, but he tried hard not to let it show. "Can I touch him?" Von asked, staring at the tube down his brother's throat.

"Yes, be careful. Keep in mind that he is in a coma, so he can't feel or hear anything. He is heavily sedated so the tubes are not uncomfortable. He is resting peacefully," Dr. Ramon advised.

He then walked out of the room, leaving the two with their loved one.

"I'm so sorry, baby bro," Von said, releasing the tears he was fighting so hard to hold onto. "Just stay with me, bro. You can't leave me now, man. I'd give anything to switch places with you right now. I promise I am going to find out who did this." The more he talked, the more his voice cracked. Von felt himself about to break, and before he did that in front of anyone, he kissed his brother on the forehead and walked out the room, leaving Nivea to grieve alone.

"What am I going to do now? I can't lose you . . . No, no, I just can't. Please wake up." Nivea cried like a baby as she held Jay's hand. She cried until her throat began to hurt and her head felt as if someone was hitting her in the head with bowling balls. Careful not to apply too much pressure, Nivea laid her head on Jay's stomach, and prayed silently, "Lord, please do not take my heart. I need him. He's my everything. Lord, I know you didn't send him to me just to take him away and leave me miserable. Please, Jay, come back to me. My life will never be the same if I lose you." Just like Jay had taught her, she closed her eyes and tried to listen for the Lord to respond.

Chapter Four

When Brandy finally made it to work, she hurried to the bathroom in the ER. She worked in ICU and knew that none of her friends or the people she worked with on a daily would be down there to see her. In the bathroom, the first thing Brandy did was lock the door behind her. Then she rushed over to the mirror and looked herself over closely to make sure that her marks were covered. She smiled at the wonderful job her Fashion Fair makeup had done.

Now satisfied and confident that she could work a normal shift without her secret being exposed, she went into her purse, pulled out a bottle of Vicodin, and popped two for the pain she was beginning to experience. She wished she had some medicine to heal her broken heart, she thought as she swallowed the pills, while looking at herself in the mirror.

I will have a great night and an even better day tomorrow, she thought as she walked out of the restroom, making her way to ICU. As she turned the corner, she bumped into a firm chest. "Excuse me," she apologized. When she looked up and realized that it was Von, her smile was as big and bright as the sun. *Wow! My night is already getting better,* she thought as she batted her eyes at a stressful looking Von. "My bad, Von, I didn't see you." She stood there staring at him.

Von recognized who she was, but he wasn't in a mood for socializing. He simply walked past Brandy and out of the hospital. Although he took note of her little flirty gesture, he had no time to address it. Fuck a bitch. He was going to find out who hurt his brother.

"Damn, he's fine," Brandy mumbled as she watched him walk off. *A chick like Coco does not deserve a good man like him.* She thought of the dude she'd seen Coco leave with from the bar one night. She'd never told her that she'd seen her, but she wanted so bad to ask her, 'If Von is all that you say, why are you stepping out on him?' But the more she hung around her, the clearer it was that Coco was just an ungrateful bitch. *I sure wouldn't mind hitting that,* Brandy thought as she walked over to the nurses' station to see if she could find out whom Von was there to see. Coco had already told her he was a bad boy, so no telling who it was.

CRSO

Coco & Dre

Dre smiled at Coco as he watched her sleeping like a baby with her thumb in her mouth. He'd given her exactly what she needed to relax and forget all about that weak-ass nigga Von. The two had smoked a half of a blunt right before Dre had made love to her. This night he'd broken his record and made sure she'd had at

98

least six orgasms before he got his. The most he'd ever given her before in one night was five. There was no denying that he had good sex. Coco couldn't even lie and say that he didn't treat her as she needed to be treated, with love and respect, but she could say that she wasn't ready to give her heart to another. Von had a hold on her.

Dre eased her out of his arms, and before getting out the bed, he planted a kiss on the back of her neck. He grabbed his cell from his pants and walked out of the room onto his balcony. Looking at his cell, he had several missed calls, but he decided to call the one back he thought was the most important.

"What's up J-Box?" he said when his homeboy answered the phone.

"Man, you ain't about to believe this, cuz." J-Box replied.

"Shit, wait until you hear this." Dre copped a seat on the chair. "That nigga Von has a twin. That's who got popped."

"Yeah, that's what I was about to tell you. Niggas thought they'd seen a ghost when cuz came through tonight."

Dre jumped from the chair. "That nigga came to our hood? Saying what?"

"Talking about that shit happened close to our hood, so we should know what the fuck was up. The little homie Bam-Bam was about to draw down on him, but one-time hit the corner. The nigga Von got away, but Bam-Bam got jacked. He had a burner on him, so you know they took him in."

"So the nigga came through my hood, sweating my homies, because his punk-ass brother got hit? Who cuz think he is?" Dre fumed. Dre went to get his other half of the blunt. When he got back in the room, Coco was getting dressed. "Let me call you right back," he told his boy and hung up.

"Why are you always running off? When are you going to stay the night with me?" He walked up and put his arms around her waist. His pipe touching her bottom gave him an instant hard on.

"I need to go get my baby." She pulled away from him. "And from what I heard, Von ain't made it home to get him." She bent down and picked up her pants from the chair. "Damn! Move!" She elbowed Dre when he tried to grab her by her thong.

"I see you're tripping again, so I'm going to leave you alone." Dre moved back. He walked over, grabbed his blunt from the ashtray, lit it, and smoked it as he watched her preparing to leave.

Before walking out of the room, she looked at Dre. "That's fucked up how you talked about Von's brother like that. The man is fighting for his life." She rolled her eyes. "Yeah, I heard you."

"I don't give a fuck about his brother!" He followed her into the living room. "And if that nigga comes to my hood again, I promise you, your baby-daddy is dead. Fuck was he doing questioning my homeboys. Nigga's got that many enemies?"

Coco shook her head and left.

CR&SO

When Coco walked in the house, to her surprise, Von was home. He and the baby were sound asleep on the coach. Coco took the baby from his arms, causing Von to wake up. He stared at Coco with a mean glare.

"Put my son down and get away from us. Go take a shower or something. I can smell that nigga's cheap-ass cologne."

Coco knew he was mad, and though Von had cheated and dissed her several times, she still felt bad about her own actions. As she placed the baby back in Von's arms, she wondered if he really could smell Dre's cologne.

"You know the nigga's broke; he's still wearing Curve," he yelled behind her.

Coco didn't say a word. She took her ass in the room and showered.

Cℜℬↄ

When Coco walked out of the living room, Von thought about following behind her and beating her ass. He knew she had been with a nigga. He could smell the cologne on her, and the fact that she didn't bother to say some slick shit when he dismissed her confirmed it. He sat there for a few minutes debating if he wanted to get up and knock her ass out or not. How in the hell did she go lay up with another nigga and his brother had just been shot? "The bitch didn't even bother to ask was he o.k."

Von rose from the couch; he laid the baby in his spot and stood up. All she could ever be was a baby momma. He could never wife her. She was too ghetto and nagged to damn much. The only reason he was still with her was because of their child. As he'd promised her when she got pregnant, "I'll stick with you 'til the wheels fall off;" and that was what he was doing. He wanted his kid to reap the benefits of having both parents in his face when he woke up in the morning and went to bed at night.

Von wasn't ever thinking about just being with one woman. He loved women and the gold they carried between their legs too much. He would do a different broad three times a day if he had the chance. That was just how he was, but he be damned if Coco was going to do it. Everything she had belonged to him—from the clothing shop she owned to the Lexus truck she drove to the house where she laid her head and the air she breathed. She was his. Von began to bite his jaw when he thought about Coco giving up what was his. She played that innocent roll to the T, but Von knew she wasn't a saint. The last few months had been telling on her, but he couldn't prove it. *I'm about to smell this hoe's thong,* he thought as he made his way upstairs to their room.

Before he got to their bedroom door, his cell went off. He pulled the phone from his pocket and looked at it. It was Chell, ol' girl from Roscoe's. Just a few hours earlier, he had been thinking about hitting her up to set up a fuck date, but he had been caught up with another broad. But not now, he wasn't in the mood. His brother had been shot and his baby-momma was up to some slick shit. Von pressed 'Ignore' on the call and put his phone back in his paints.

When he walked into the bedroom, he could hear the shower running and smell sweet pea body wash in the air. Von walked into the bathroom and snatched the shower curtain open.

Coco jumped. "Boy, you scared me." She held her heart.

"Where are the panties you took off?" He stared at her with that evil glare.

"What?" she answered, unsure if she had heard him right.

"You heard what the fuck I said. Where are the panties you took off?"

Oh shit, this fool is crazy. Coco's heart rate began to increase.

"I'm not going to ask you again," he warned.

When Coco noticed Von biting the inside of his jaw, she knew he was serious. She slowly reached her hand up and grabbed her underwear from the top of the shower door.

"Here, Von." She handed them to him.

He snatched them from her hands. "Since when did you start washing your panties by hand?" He flinched at her like he was about to hit her. Coco covered her face.

"Stop, Von, you're tripping. Get out."

Von was pissed off. He took the panties and threw them at her. He then began to slap her across the head, causing her to fall on the shower floor.

"What is wrong with you?" she cried.

"Bitch, shut your ass up. I know you've been with a nigga."

"No, I haven't." Coco was still on the floor, covering her head.

"Stop lying." He reached down and slapped her again. The water from the shower had him all wet, but he didn't give a damn. He was furious.

"Stop . . . Stop . . ." Coco cried.

"Fuck you," he said, after the last slap to her back. He stood there staring her. He thought about making her have sex with him; but the hurt he had, not knowing if he would lose his brother, and the anger in him, knowing that Coco had stepped out with another, he couldn't even get hard.

"You can't turn a ho into a housewife," were his last words before leaving out of the bathroom, on out the front door. Wet and all, he needed to get away and clear his mind.

Von's words hurt Coco more than the hits. She couldn't believe he flipped like that, after all the shit he had done.

Chapter Five

Two weeks had gone by, and Coco and Von had barely spoken to each other. Between him running the streets, and going back and forth to the hospital, she rarely saw him. Von had been running so much, he didn't have time to chill with his son, and that wasn't cool at all. So Sunday was the day he decided to chill at his and Coco's place with his baby boy.

Coco was surprised to see that, at one in the afternoon, Von was relaxed on the couch with Little Von, watching the game. She didn't question it; she just played the wifey role by making the best of it. Coco showered and changed into a cute little T and boy-short set from VS. Normally, when she was just lying around the house, she didn't bother to undo her wrap, but she wanted to give Von something good to look at so she let her hair down. She even did her makeup, but instead of putting on lipstick, she dressed her lips in strawberry lip gloss. She sprayed on a little body spray and dabbed behind her ears with Angel by VS. She started to put on heels, but thought that was overdoing it and slid on a pair of flip-flops.

As she was walking out of the room, her cell rang. It was Dre. She rolled her eyes and sent him to voicemail. "Damn, nigga, don't you get the hint? I don't like you," Coco mumbled as she tossed the cell in the drawer. Coco hadn't talk to Dre since the night Jay had been shot, and she didn't want to. She didn't appreciate his actions the last time that they were together. On her way into the kitchen, Coco saw Von and the baby snacking on a sandwich.

"I'm about to cook dinner," said Coco as she walked into the kitchen.

Von looked up at her as she walked in the kitchen. Upon seeing her ass hanging from her shorts, he licked his lips and his second head began to throb. He hadn't had any in over two weeks. It surprised him, but there was so much shit going on, he hadn't had time; but now he was going to make time. He tried giving the baby the last little piece of the sandwich, but he turned his head, so Von ate it himself. He then picked up the baby, laid him on his chest, and began trying to put him to sleep. His was getting an erection as he thought about getting some of Coco's warm honey.

In the kitchen, Coco took out a package of chicken and sat it on the counter. She pulled a couple of cans of cream of mushroom soup from the cabinet and a bag of rice. She put the frozen chicken in the microwave to defrost, then reached in the cabinet to get a couple of pots. She hadn't noticed that Von had been watching her until she felt his arms wrap around her waist; she couldn't help but smile. Instead of responding as he was grinding on her buttocks, she continued to pull out the last pot.

"Mmmm," she moaned when Von slid her shorts to the side and inserted two of his fingers inside of her.

"You want me, don't you?" he whispered in her ear.

Coco nodded her head in agreement as he began to toy with her love box. She tightened up her walls on his fingers and began to move her ass in a circular motion on his manhood. She could feel the growing evidence of his arousal hardness. Von's warm breath sent chills down her back. The way he used his thumb to play with her pearl as he stroked in and out of her, she was right at the peak of cumming.

"Shhhh . . . oh . . . ah . . . yesss."

Brrrr Brrrr

Von's cell began to vibrate. Coco didn't know whether Von would answer or not, so she gave him a head's up.

"Baby, I'm about to cum," Coco squealed, rotating her hips at a faster pace. Von moved his fingers to match her pace and applied more pressure to her swollen clit. "Ohhhh shit, daddy, oh shit . . ." she cried. With his free hand, Von dropped his basketball shorts, and his rod stood at attention. He lifted her T-shirt up, yanked her shorts down, ripped her G-string off, and jammed his hardness inside of her.

"Damn Co..." He thrust in and out of her, increasing the tempo.

Brrrr Brrrr

His cell went off again. Coco ignored it. As if she was fighting for the win, she rocked back on Von with all she had, hoping that he wouldn't stop. She didn't want to miss this much-needed orgasm.

"Babbbby . . ." Coco was breathing hard. "Ohhhh, baby, you feel so good . . . Ohhhh . . . Don't stop," she begged, as the loud-ass house phone began to ring. "Ohhhh, Vonnnn . . ." Coco was almost there.

Von was still giving it to her, but he wasn't really focused. His mind was on the ringing phones. He thought that it had to be an emergency. It might not have been a coincidence that both his cell and house phones were ringing back-to-back. Just as he was debating on whether to tell Coco to hold on, the answering machine picked up. 'You've reached Coco and Von. Leave a message after the beep.' Coco was focusing on her nut while Von's mind was on who was calling back-to-back. "Coco, can you or Von call the hospital. This is Brandy."

With his pants still down, Von ran over and picked up the phone. "S'up, Brandy? This is Von."

He was a little out of breath, which told Brandy why they weren't answering their phones. As Von listened to what Brandy was telling him, Coco pulled up her shorts, rolled her eyes, picked up her G-string and threw them in the trash, and went to check on the baby, who was crying.

"Where you going," Coco asked when Von walked in the living room grabbing his car keys.

"Brandy said Nivea hasn't been home since she came yesterday morning. All she does is cry." He walked over, gave Coco a kiss, then kissed his little man on the forehead.

"So how are you going to make her go home?" Coco rolled her eyes thinking, *Since when had he and the bitch become close?*

"Don't start that dumb shit," was all he said, and he left.

Von and Nivea had kind of been each other's support since Jay had been shot. He had been checking on her, she had checked on him, and they had taken turns being at the hospital with Jay, with Nivea there the most. She had even begun to loosen up, and she and Von were able to have a decent conversation without arguing or criticizing the other, something they couldn't do in the past. They were becoming cool, and Von knew that his brother would have wanted it that way.

When Von walked into the hospital room and saw Nivea standing over Jay crying, he immediately walked over and placed his arm around her shoulders. He wasn't expecting Nivea to react how she did; but when she turned and buried her face on his chest, he just rubbed her back. As he watched his brother lying there, debating whether he wanted to come back to them or not, he continued to whisper that everything would be all right.

Chapter Six

Coco had finished cooking dinner, fed the baby, played with him for a little while, bathed and put him to bed, and Von still hadn't shown up or returned her calls. She had called him at least three times. She wanted to call more, but since he was with his brother, she didn't. But it was nine o'clock now and visiting hours were over. *Where in the hell are you?* Coco thought. She shook her head at the thought of him being in the streets. "He could have brought his ass back and had dinner, or at least called," she said as she walked over and picked up the house phone to call Brandy. Brandy didn't answer so Coco left her a message to call back ASAP.

CR80

"Hello?" Coco answered the phone.

"What's up, Coco? It's me," said Brandy, calling her back from the hospital phone.

"Hey, girl, is everything okay with JayVon? How is he?"

"No change, but his vitals are good, so that's a good thing."

"That's good. He's strong; he'll pull through. How is Nivea? Is she still up there?"

"No, she and Von left like two hours ago. When he came, he was able to convince her to leave." Brandy paused. "I wonder if he came back to get her car?" she said, more to herself than Coco.

"What's wrong with her car?" asked Coco.

"Nothing, I assume she was just too out of it to drive. Girl, she looked a mess. I feel so sorry for her. JayVon must be a really good man. When Von came, she broke down in his arms. I see why you love him. He is a thug, but so sweet. It brought tears to my eyes to see how he was consoling her. I could tell he was trying to prevent himself from breaking down," Brandy said all in one breath. "Hello? Are you there?" Brandy removed the phone from her ear and looked at it. Placing the phone back on her ear, she heard Coco speak.

"Yeah, I'm here. That's the baby crying. Let me call you back, or you call me when you get off."

Coco hung up without even saying bye. She then tried Von again, and when he didn't answer, her next call was to the neighbor to see if she would babysit.

"No, I can't. I have company. Sorry, honey," her neighbor replied.

"No problem. Thanks anyway." Coco hung up the phone. *I guess he'll be going with me,* she thought, referring to Little Von. Coco ran up the stairs and changed into pants and a tank top. Then she grabbed the baby along with his blanket. It was time to make that mission.

CRSO

Von

Knock Knock Knock

Ding Dong . . . Ding Dong . . .

The faint knocking at the door and the ringing of the doorbell caused him to shift in his sleep. Not fully awake, he lay there a minute and tried to focus on what he was hearing.

When he moved, a cool breeze from the night air found its way in, causing Nivea to scoot closer to him and bury her face in his chest. She wrapped her arms around him and intertwined her legs with his. She wanted to keep the warmth from his body heat. Nivea knew that at any moment the alarm clock would sound off, alerting him that it was time to get up to get ready for work. Monday through Friday, it was the same routine. She hated for him to leave her in bed alone; if she had it her way, she would stay cuddled in his love forever.

BAM BAM BAM

The knocking turned into loud banging, causing them to jump up. Thinking that it was the police, or maybe the niggas who had shot his brother had followed him, Von hopped out of bed. He grabbed his boxers and sweat pants from the floor, and put them on. He went over to the chair where his hoodie was lying, and grabbed the gun tucked underneath. He looked over at Nivea.

Dammit! Who could be knocking this early in the morning, Nivea thought.

"Grab your robe and stay here. I'm about to go see who's at the door. Don't come out until I give you the o.k."

Nivea eyes bulged; that wasn't her husband's voice. She quickly looked to her left, and her eyes threatened to pop out of her head. Realization sank in, and she was immediately ashamed when she realized that she was with her husband's brother.

"Are you just going to sit there and stare at me, or are you going to get your ass up and get dressed? There ain't no telling who that could be at the door," Von said, looking at her with a hurry-your-ass-up face.

The knocks continued to get louder and louder. Nivea jumped up out of the bed, trying to cover her body up. She was feeling naked, not because she *was* naked, but because she had been hit with the naked truth. She had slept with her husband's twin brother. When she tried to walk, the soreness between her legs confirmed what she already knew.

"Hurry the fuck up, Niv, and get dressed! I'm going to see who the fuck is at the door."

With his gun in his hand, Von hurried out of the room. He ran down the stairs, taking them two at a time; he was ready. He made it downstairs and peeped through the peephole. Damn! It was Coco! *Shit,* he thought as he ran back up the stairs to get Nivea.

What the hell have you done, Nivea? How could you? she questioned herself as she walked into the bathroom. The guilt began to sink in, and she felt so dirty. She wanted to crawl up under the sink and hide. *How did this happen,* she thought as she turned on the cold water and threw some on her face.

CRƎD

She remembered being at the hospital, begging Jay to wake up, and telling him how much she needed him. Then Von had come, and after breaking down in his arms, he was finally able to convince her to allow him to drive her home. "What about my car," she had asked.

"After I get you settled, I will call one of my boys to follow me to get your car."

"Ok," she said, then walked over to her husband and kissed him good night. Nivea was so out of it on the ride home that she hadn't even noticed she was in her driveway until Von was standing on her side of the door, asking her to get out.

In the house, Nivea and Von sat there for about thirty minutes, chatting and daydreaming for the most part. To Von, Nivea seemed cool, so he told her he was about to go. Besides, Coco was blowing his phone up, and he was still horny.

"Nivea, call me if you need me. I'm about to go home." Von stood up.

"Please, Von . . . Um . . . Do you have to leave this second? I don't want to be in this big house alone. Please don't leave right now. It's just . . . well . . . I'm so used to JayVon being here with me." Tears began to fall from her eyes. She added, "That's the reason these last two weeks that I've stayed at the hospital. Well, that and because I miss him so much. I just have to be next to him. Von, I don't know what I'm going to do without him." Then she broke down crying hysterically.

Von understood how much she was hurting, and he wished that he could take her pain away. He wished that he could go back and change that night, and that he had gone to get the wings. He wished that it was him fighting for his life. He couldn't change what had happened, and he couldn't take his brother's wife's pain away; all he could do was be there.

Von walked over to Nivea and wrapped his arms around her. "Shhhh . . . It's cool. I won't leave. I'll chill with you for a minute."

Hearing those words, Nivea wiped her tears. She looked up at him, smiled, and said, "Thank you," while thinking, Damn! He looks like my baby. *She removed herself from his arms. "Make yourself comfortable," she offered.*

Von did just that. He walked over to the LA-Z Boy and took a seat, grabbing the remote in the process.

Nivea was grateful for Von's kind gesture. "Would you like anything to drink?" she asked.

"Yeah, Henny on the rocks, no chaser," he said as he flipped through the channels.

Nivea walked over to the bar and made his drink. As she handed it to him, she asked, "Are you hungry?" She chuckled, thinking about what she had just asked. She thought back to the day when she had tried to cook the chicken, and Von had come in there clowning her about having Shake 'N Bake.

"Nah, the last time I wanted you to feed me, you damn near burned down the house." They shared a much-needed laugh.

"Forget you. I am going to shower, if you don't mind?"

"Naw, go ahead. I may make me a sandwich or something."

"Sure enough," Nivea replied, and headed to her room.

As Nivea walked into the room, the scent of JayVon's cologne lingered in the air, reminding her that, even when he wasn't present, he was still there. Nivea closed her eyes and inhaled as much as she could of his cologne. "I miss you, baby," she whispered, as she looked over to the nightstand, where a picture of them on their wedding night sat. Her eyes instantly filled with tears as she walked over and picked up the picture, first kissing it, then placing it close to her heart.

After a few moments, she sat the picture back down and sat on her bed. She picked up Jay's pillow, brought it up to her nose, and inhaled his scent. Nivea sat there a few moments with her thoughts before laying the pillow back down and walking into her master bathroom. Nivea was in need of a long, hot shower to relax. She would rather take a long, hot bubble bath, but she didn't want to leave Von downstairs alone for that long.

CRSD

Nivea stepped out the shower, feeling a little more relaxed than before. Before stepping out of the bathroom, she dried her body and hair, then wrapped the towel around her head. In the bedroom, she took her Oil of Olay lotion and walked over to her California King, where she sat down and moisturized her body. As she thought about how she and Jay would massage each other after their baths or showers, her clit began to throb. A smile spread across her face when she thought of how their massages had turned into sweet lovemaking. As Nivea rubbed her perky breasts, her nipples began to harden, causing her to yearn for her husband's touch even more.

"Please wake up, honey, please wake up. Oh God, oh how I miss you," she whispered with her eyes closed.

Standing up and walking over to dresser, she placed the Olay back in its original spot and pulled open the top drawer. Thinking of being comfortable, she took out a tank top and slid it on. Then she opened the second drawer, grabbed her short shorts, and put them on. Unwrapping the towel from around her hair, she folded it, set it on the edge of the bed, and headed back downstairs, leaving her hair loose and wet.

When Nivea got downstairs, Von was no longer relaxing on the La-Z Boy, but lying on her couch. Any other time, she would never have allowed company to do such thing, but with all that was going on, it was too petty to address. Nivea noticed Von's empty glass on the floor. *"Do you want a refill?"* she asked, grabbing his glass and heading towards the bar to make herself a drink as well.

"Yeah," he said as his eyes followed her to the bar, where she now stood making their drinks. The pink tank top she was wearing without a bra made it obvious that her nipples were hard. Von had to sit up straight and re-adjust himself. Damn! he thought, his mind drifting back to what he and Coco had had going on back at the house. At the sound of Regina King's voice, Von turned his head and focused back on the movie he was watching, Poetic Justice. *"That's some cold shit."* He laughed and shook his head. Iesha was clowning Chicago about him not being able to fuck, and how she was fucking someone else.

Nivea walked from the bar with the glasses. *"Here you go,"* she said, handing him a glass of Henny on the rocks. She looked over at the television and shook her head. Yes, they're twins, she thought. Poetic Justice *was also her husband's favorite movie, and he would laugh at the same part.*

"Damn, girl, I thought you had fallen asleep, you took so long, I was about to sneak out after the movie went off." Von took a sip of his drink. His eyes were still fixed on the TV.

"Oh no, I'm sorry. I'm glad you didn't. I just needed to relax." She took a sip of her drink and continued talking. "All of the running back and forth to the hospital, talking with the different doctors, and trying to keep it together, has totally drained me. I really needed to come home and sleep. I just didn't want to leave his side, you know?"

"I understand, but he needs you to rest as well. When he comes home, you're going to need all of your energy to take care of him." Von didn't care what anyone said; his brother was coming home and soon.

Talking about JayVon, Nivea could feel herself going back into a funk, and she didn't want that, so she changed the subject. Nivea began to talk about the good times. They laughed and joked around, had a few more drinks in between the conversation, then continued watching the movie. She learned things about Von that she'd never known before. He wasn't as bad as she'd thought. Listening to him talk, she concluded that he was intelligent like his brother. He had just got caught up in the street life, and Jay had chosen to get out.

Talking on a more serious note, Nivea decided that it was a good time to address a few things. After how she treated Von, not just at the hospital but also over the years, she thought it would be a great time to apologize.

"Um . . . Von, I truly appreciate you keeping me company. I want to apologize for judging you before I really got to know you. We never really sat down and talked, so I admit I was wrong. I'm sorry for everything I said to you at the hospital." She took a deep breath, feeling awful. As she lifted her head and looked into his eyes, she could see the hurt. "I was hurting, Von, and I needed to blame someone, so I blamed you."

Turning back to the TV, he said, "Nah, it's cool. This shit would have never fuckin' happened to him if I wasn't in the streets. I just wish I could take your pain away and change places with him."

Seeing him getting upset and hearing the pain in his voice, Nivea scooted closer to him. She placed her hand on his shoulder. "It not your fault, Von; you didn't pull the trigger."

Von's eyes became watery. Hearing her talk about the person who had pulled the trigger and fact that he had no leads on who had gunned him down, really tore him apart on the inside. He didn't reply to Nivea's comment, he just kept staring at the television. By this time, the movie had ended, and Janet Jackson singing Anytime Anyplace was blaring through the surround system.

Nivea saw that Von was holding back tears, and felt the need to hug him. Nivea stood up and moved closer to him. Placing both knees on the couch and sitting on her legs, she wrapped her arms around his neck. "It's o.k. to let it out, Von. I'm here for you. We need to have each other's back."

Being so close to him, smelling his cologne, feeling the effects of the two glasses of Henny, and listening to Janet's soft tunes, had her feeling things she knew were wrong. With her breasts pressed against him, she whispered in a sexy tone in his ear, "Von, I need you, pleasssse," she begged, as her hands began to glide down his back and back up to his broad shoulders.

He felt so good to her, with his firm chest against her pulsing nipples. She was missing the touch of a man, "her man." It was wrong, but with him being identical to her husband, she needed him to fulfill what her husband couldn't at that moment. The fire between her legs needed to be put out in the worst way.

Von sat quietly, trying to register what she was asking of him, as she began to tickle his neck with her tongue.

Nivea continued to seduce him, blowing and passionately twirling her tongue on his ear. In between making a pattern of kisses from his neck around to the corner of his lips, she begged him again. "Please, Von . . . Kiss me. We both need this. Don't fight us," she said, referring to herself and his growing arousal that she noticed poking through his pants. Anxious to touch him, she began to slide her hand down to his mid-section. Just when she was about to go a little farther, he grabbed her hands, yanking her off him.

"What the fuck are you doing, Nivea?" His voice boomed over the music.

He was pissed that she had him horny, causing an erection. He didn't want to feel what he was feeling for his brother's wife. He knew that this would be the ultimate betrayal. This shit was a no-no. Growing up, they may have slept with each other girlfriends—because those bitches didn't mean shit to either one of them—but they had an understanding on whom not to cross the line with—Nivea and Coco were it.

Nivea, not one to be rejected, continued to seduce him. She stood up directly in front of him and took a couple steps back. She looked into his eyes as she slowly lifted her top over her breasts and over her head, allowing it to drop on floor. She knew she wasn't playing fair, but when she wanted something, she was going to get it.

Nivea's body was like a fine wine. Men would go out of their way, at any expense, to buy her and drink her right up. Von couldn't believe Nivea would take it this far. Staring at her, he was torn between a rock hard-on, Nivea's video vixen body, and the thought of betraying his brother. Trying to make the right decision, he stood up to leave, but she walked right up on his sleek, slender body with its fine, musculature form.

She wasted no time grabbing his swollen, throbbing shaft, and began massaging it through his pants. She was creaming between her lips, and she be damned if she was going to let him get away. She knew he had plenty of women fighting over him, and judging by his size, she understood why.

"Let me make you feel good," she said, as she dropped down to her knees, yanking his sweats down, and coming face-to-face with his erection. Her mouth watered up. "Relax, we both need this," she told him hungrily, as she wrapped her mouth around his fullness in a state of desperation. She used her hands to glide up and down the length of it, as her tongue caressed the head. Relaxing the muscles in her throat, she pushed as much of him down her throat as she could.

Von's mind left out the door and went home to his baby-momma, but his feet never moved. The visual he got watching Nivea deep throat him could have driven anyone off a cliff. "Ahhhh, damn!" he moaned.

Nivea stopped at nothing. She pulled out all the tricks. She was what you called a true man-eater. She moaned, teased, sucked, and licked him clean. "Ohhhh, yessss . . . Mmmm," she said, licking her lips, "you taste so good."

Von wrapped his hand in her hair, guiding her head. That's it, she thought, happy that he was no longer resisting what was bound to happen. Then, all of a sudden, he yanked her head back, and wrapped his other hand around her neck, pulling her up. He was pissed off, but it was undeniable that the lust was there, and Von couldn't fight it. He backed up her against the wall and hungrily kissed her lips, capturing her mouth with an urgency, and worked his way down to her beautifully-formed breasts.

"Yessss . . . Vonnnn . . . Ohhhh yessss . . ." More moans escaped from her mouth.

He stopped, threw his shirt over his head, and ripped her shorts off. He was like an outraged bull.

"I want you to fuck me, Von," she said, ready to attack him with just as much vigor.

Von was so frustrated; he needed a release, and since Nivea wanted to volunteer the goods, he was determined to beat it out of commission. He lifted her up, placing her directly on his rod, and forced his way right in. Taking both of his hands, cuffing them under her butt, he displayed his power and strength as he aggressively bounced her up and down on him.

Nivea didn't know if she was coming or going. Von was putting a beat-down on her. She had no idea what she had gotten herself into. She began to scream out as she wrapped her legs around his waist and went on the ride of her life.

"Oh Von, youuuu . . . ahhhh . . . ye young me tong teehe, so bigggg," she said, babbling. Her stomach knotted up. "Ohhhh, yessss. I'm . . . cummmminnnn . . . ahhhhh."

After her orgasm, he carried her around, still bouncing her up and down. You could see the muscles flex in his long, dark, glistening legs as the sweat ran down them from the workout he was giving Nivea.

"Damn girl," he said, embedding himself deeply in her tight walls. Von whispered sweet nothings as soft groans escaped his mouth. He carried her over to the arm of the couch and sat her down, ready to go in deeper.

Nivea arched her back as Von held her with one hand, and squeezed her breast with the other. "Ohhhh . . . Von, you feel so good. Harder, harder. Punish me!" she begged. Von began to speed up the pace, nearing his orgasm. "Cum for me!" he demanded, and just like that, she shot out.

But he wasn't done. It was her turn to put in the work. While still inside of her, he sat on the couch and allowed her to take a few seconds to catch her breath. She looked into Von's eyes. "No one has ever made me cum so hard." She brought her lips to his, and his tongue slid between her parted lips and found hers. He stroked her mouth to ecstasy, causing her to start rotating her hips. It became very intense as she connected with him on a level that she never had with her husband; that caused her to buck and ride the wild and wonderful waves of sheer ecstasy.

"Damn, Niv . . . Shit!" He was almost there, and she knew it, so she planted both feet on the couch and sank herself down on him again and again and again. Von didn't like the feeling of not being in control, so he gripped her hips tight, slamming her down on him. With every stroke, the pain was almost unbearable. When that final moment came, Von flooded himself into her, moaning and groaning.

Nivea lay on the couch, weaker than she'd ever been. Von didn't say a word. He just stood, pulled his pants back up, picked her up, and carried her upstairs for another three rounds. And, that was just the beginning. Nivea didn't know it, but she was officially addicted.

CRIED

Bam Bam Bam

"Von, open this muthafuckin door right now! I know you hear me," Coco shouted, bringing Nivea back to reality. Before she could figure out what to do, Von stormed into the room. "Nivea," he called out, "it's Coco." Nivea covered her face and shook her head at the thought of facing the number-one drama queen.

What in the fuck is going on in there? thought Coco, as she stood at the door waiting for someone to answer. "Von! Von! You hear me . . . It's dark out here. Open the door." She continued to knock. Then a thought crossed her mind. *Maybe he left to go get her car.* She stepped off the porch to look up at the second-story windows. When she saw the light come on in the room, she began to scream both Nivea and Von's names. She was about to make an even bigger scene if that door didn't open and fast.

"I do have neighbors."

Coco looked up, and Nivea was standing on the porch. Coco walked back toward the porch. "Where's Von?" Coco asked, looking her up and down. The bitch was fully dressed, but looked as if she had just awakened. *What the fuck is really going on?*

"Von, I know you can hear her. Coco is out here. Please do something." Nivea looked behind her at Von, who was sitting across the way in the family room watching TV. "Come in, I guess," said Nivea.

As Nivea walked away from the door, her heart was thumping so hard it threatened to burst through her chest. The anxiety coming from her reality was slowly draining her. Not only had she slept with JayVon's twin while he was on his deathbed, but she was almost caught by Von's baby-momma.

"Lock the door behind you," Nivea said, as she walked past the family room and back up the stairs.

Coco walked up on Von and placed her hands on her hips. "What's going on? I've been calling you. Why in the fuck didn't y'all answer the door?"

"If she didn't answer the door, how did you get in?" Von never looked up at Coco; he continued to act as if he was focused on the news.

"Well, what took so long?" She shifted her body weight to one side. Her eyes narrowed on an item under the sofa.

"I fell asleep. Damn, Coco, don't come over here with that shit!" He looked up at her. "And what was so important that you come over here banging on the door at this time of night?" Von looked up at her, and noticed her nose flaring and her lip jumping.

Von knew what was up. She was pissed, so he tried to deter her again by asking about his son. "Who the fuck is watching my son while you're over here acting stupid?"

"He's safe," she snapped. She wasn't about to tell him that, at that moment, he was sleeping in the car. Naw, she had her own questions. "What's that?" Her index finger was shaking as she pointed to the item.

Von opened his legs and looked down. "What's what?" He didn't see anything.

Coco pushed his legs out of the way, bent over, pulled Nivea's shorts from under the couch, and dangled them in the air. "Why in the hell are these under the couch? The same couch you were sitting on?"

"What the fuck do you mean? This is her house. Shit, maybe she forgot to clean up. Ask her." Von stared at the shorts in Coco's hands as if he didn't know how they had gotten there—like he hadn't just taken them off her a couple of hours prior.

"No, I'm asking you. In fact, where is the hoe? Maybe she won't mind telling the truth." She turned to walk in the direction Nivea had gone, but Von grabbed her by the arm and snatched her back.

"Don't you even bring your stupid ass over here with that bullshit!" He was so close in her face that she could smell the tart on his breath. "Are you that fucking insecure that you're trying to make assumptions that something's going on with me and my brother's wife?"

He took his thumb and flicked the tip of his nose. As Coco watched him bite the inside of his jaw, she thought that maybe she had taken it too far this time. She prayed he didn't knock the hell out of her for her stupid thoughts.

"Let me get the fuck out of here before I lay your ass out," he warned her.

Von flinched at her and Coco jumped. He shook his head and grabbed his keys off the table. "Niv, I'm gone," he yelled as he walked out the house.

Nivea was standing at the top of the stairs, listening to everything. She prayed that Coco didn't come up the stairs.

"Von . . . Von . . ." she heard Coco call after her baby-daddy, then the door slammed.

Nivea ran over to the window in the hallway and watched Coco try to make Von talk to her. She couldn't hear the words that were being said; but the way Von jumped up out of his truck, got

134

up in her face, and Coco walked off to her truck, she figured out what was going on. Nivea hurried and ran down the stairs to lock her doors. She then dropped to her knees and began to sob. "I'm just like my mother," she cried. "Baby, forgive me. JayVon, I am so sorry."

Chapter Seven

Nivea

The guilt was eating her up so much that Nivea didn't even bother to go see her husband. Although he wasn't conscious, and probably didn't know that she was there, she couldn't face him. It was too much. So instead of spending her day at the hospital, she decided to go see her father.

Mr. Banner had been a widow for eight years, but single for twelve. Nivea's mother had left him when Nivea graduated from high school. She had never officially moved out, but she had lived her own life with a man who was ten years younger than she was. Nivea had been devastated when she found out what her mother was doing to her father, and shocked to learn that it wasn't the first time. Her mother had always cheated on her father, and pitiful as it was, she'd driven him to drinking, which had eventually caused him to lose his job.

The good thing was that their house was paid off, and after her mother had passed away from a brain tumor, Mr. Banner had collected a nice sum of money from the insurance policy, which Nivea had power of attorney over. She had forced him into rehab and, after successful completion of the twelve-step program, he had been sober for the last five years. Because the loss of her mother still affected him, he had refused to move on. Quiet as it's kept, the only reason he stayed strong was for Nivea.

Mr. Banner was sitting in his favorite chair, reading the paper and drinking his noonday cup of coffee, when he heard Nivea let herself in.

"Hi, Daddy," Nivea said. She walked over and kissed him on the forehead.

He looked up from the paper and smiled. "How was your visit with my son-in-law?"

"Good," she lied. She knew that if she told her dad that she hadn't seen him, he would ask why and she didn't have a good excuse.

"Is everything alright with you?" Mr. Banner set his paper to the side, on the coffee table.

"Yes, Daddy." She smiled at her handsome father. Mr. Banner had the features of Denzel Washington. Women were forever telling him how handsome he was and flirting with him. He was a very good man who took care of his family. She didn't understand how her mother had refused to appreciate him. She always thought her mother was lucky to have her father. Now here she was, committing the same foolish act. Mr. Banner stared at his daughter and thought he knew exactly what was bothering her.

"He will pull through. That man won't leave you. He loves you. I've watched the way he stares at you when you're not looking. The smile he has when you laugh, the way he holds you in his arms. It's the same way I use to look at your mother. I see it. Baby, he isn't going anywhere. That man is going to make it just for you."

"Ohhhh, Daddy." Nivea burst into tears. She ran over, dropped down in front of him, laid her head on his lap, and cried.

Chapter Eight

Brandy

"Mommy, Mommy, sing, sing," Robert, Jr. said as he pointed at the set of three baby swings on the playground.

"I know just what you want, you little stinker. Don't you know Mommy knows her baby? Yes, she does," Brandy said, picking him up and planting kisses all over his face. She carried him over to the swings, placing his little legs in the holes, then strapping him in. "Now sit back, put your left hand on here, your right hand here, and hold on tight so momma can push you." After wrapping both of his little hands around the chains on the swing, she stood behind him and lightly placed her hand on his back. "Are you ready, momma's little stinky butt?" She began to push him. "Pump your feet. Pump your feet. Yeah, that's it, big boy." She smiled.

"Wheeee . . . wheeee . . . wheeee . . ." he giggled. Moments like this were what Brandy lived for. Junior was the reason she got up every day, looking forward to another life. He was the reason she worked so much overtime. It was to make sure that he had everything that he needed. She wanted to be the best mother ever, just like her mom was.

Growing up, Brandy's mom had worked as a housekeeper up to the day she'd been killed in a hit-and-run accident at a stop sign. Six months later, the cops had found out that her stepfather had purposely done it. Her mom had become tired of their abusive relationship and wanted out. The idea didn't sit well with her stepfather, so he had killed her. Brandy had been distraught.

She and her mother had always been very close. Just as Junior was the love of Brandy's life, Brandy had been the love of her mother's life. She had worked her tail off for her daughter. Although her mother's job may not have paid well, she loved what she did and spoke proudly about it. She was grateful to receive the income to be able take care of her baby girl. There were times that Brandy had known her mother had gone a couple days without eating because food was scarce, but Brandy couldn't remember a day that she had missed a meal. That was one of the many good memories she had of her mother that she held deep in her heart, and it made her want to always keep pushing to do the best she could for her child—no matter how hard life got.

"Okay, Mommy, I want to get out now."

"Sure, baby." Brandy stopped the swing and took him out. As soon as she placed him on the ground, he took off running,

"Catch me, Mommy, catch me."

"The tickle monster is here. I'm going to tickle you." She allowed him to get a little distance before she ran after him. Once she caught up with him, she swiped him up off his feet. As if he was a football, she cradled him in her left arm and began to tickle his neck. Junior could barely catch his breath he was laughing so hard. Brandy dropped to her knees, laid him on his back in the grass, and tickled him some more.

Before they knew it, the sun was beginning to go down. Brandy began to pack up Junior's toys to leave. The hour of happiness she had just experienced was replaced with bitterness. Neither she nor Junior was ready to go home, but Brandy knew the consequences if she wasn't there to prepare and serve Rob's dinner at a decent hour.

"Come on, hurry baby," Brandy told her son as she hurried the car. She sighed at the thought of going home to Robert. She never knew what mood he would be in. Most of the time, he would complain about any little thing, so he could put his hands on her. Then there were times when he was sweet, like the first day they'd met. He would apologize for beating on her and promise to never hit her again, only to do it all over—either that same day or a couple of days later.

By the time Brandy made it to the house, Junior was asleep in his car seat, with a lollipop in his hand. After parking the car, she took out her phone, took a picture of him, and smiled. Junior was so adorable with a head full of curly hair. He had his father's big brown, dreamy eyes, but those chubby cheeks and button nose came from his mother.

"Come on, big boy," she said, taking him out the car seat to carry him inside the house.

"Hey, baby, how's the king's 'big girl'?" Rob asked, looking at her wide hips as she walked through the door, carrying Junior to his bed.

"I'm fine," she said, wondering how she was going to break the news to him that he would have to watch the baby because she didn't have enough money to pay for daycare this week. After she put Junior down on the bed, she went into his bathroom, took his face cloth, and ran it under the warm water. Then she went back into the bedroom to clean him up.

"Wait a minute, sleepyhead, Mommy needs to wipe this sticky candy off you; then I'll let you sleep." Junior had placed both hands on his face, with his eyes shut tight, and kept swiping her hand away. "Okay, okay, all done," she said, smiling and giving up the battle to clean him as well as she wanted to. She took off his Blue's Clues light-up shoes, pants, and shirt, and placed them in his dirty-clothes basket. Then she put his shoes on the baby shoe rack hanging from his closet door. Walking back over to him, she knelt down, pulled the sheet over him, and kissed him on the forehead before leaving out.

"Here we go," she huffed at the sound of Rob's voice calling her name.

"Brandy, come here baby."

Taking a deep breath before closing the door behind her, she walked into the living room to see what he wanted. *Sitting on the couch with the remote in his hand,* Brandy thought, *not only is he lazy, but he surely looks it, too; just like a lazy, couch potato.* She walked over to him and stood in front of him "Yes?"

Pulling her down on his lap, he asked, "Are you still mad at me? You know I'm sorry, baby. I'm going to get help. I'mma love you until death do us part."

Thinking about what had happened to her mother, she knew that statement could be true, but with a very different meaning.

"I just get upset when you do lil shit to make me mad. You know how I am. Why do you have to do that? I know I say this all the time, but I mean it this time," he said, looking into her eyes.

"I'm going to stop hitting you. One day, I wanna make you my wife."

Staring back at him, tears begin to roll down her cheeks. She was use to the same old line. She use to believe it; but now, three years and one child later, she realized it was all lies from the beginning. She did love him and wanted him to do right by her, for once. All she had ever asked of him was for him to work, take care of his son, and take care of home.

He wiped the tears from her eyes, and asked, "Why are you crying, B? You don't want to be with me anymore? Huh? We can get past this; we always do. Baby, I promise to do better."

Brandy silently cried even harder because, as bad as she wanted to leave him, another part of her wanted to take a chance. She felt that she deserved more from him since she'd stuck it out all this time, taking the abuse and all for three years. At some point, she knew he would change. She knew there had to be a better man somewhere on the inside. She kept telling herself that, even though the truth had already revealed itself.

Rob didn't understand himself why he got so mad and beat her as he did. He knew that he felt good knowing he was in control, but afterwards, he felt bad when he saw the results of his actions. "Shhh, don't cry, baby," he said as squeezed her tight, pulling her into his chest. He stood up holding her in his arms, turned around, and laid her on the couch. He pulled her pants down, then his gym shorts, and climbed on top of her as he continued to whisper, "I love you, baby. I'm going to do right by you, I promise. I'm going to take care of you," he said right before finding his way into her warmth.

Brandy cried harder as he slowly pumped in out of her, until her cries became moans of pleasure. Minutes later, she found herself holding his face tightly and passionately kissing him, while grinding her hips to match his rhythm.

"I love you, too, baby, and no matter what, I ain't going anywhere," she confessed.

Hearing her say that she was going to be there forever, caused him to thrust in and out of her faster, until they climaxed. Just like that, all was forgiven. She was ready to give him another try, regardless of what her inner voice said.

ରଞ୍ଜେ

Now, feeling a little better, Brandy stood over the stove cooking steaks, baked potatoes, and broccoli with cheese, while singing her favorite song by Alicia Keys. *I keep on fallin' In and out of love with you I never loved someone They way that I'm lovin' you Oh baby I, I, I, I'm fallin'* . Brandy had a lovely voice, but not too many people knew it because she kept that gift to herself most of the time. For some reason, she was shy when it came to singing in front of people.

Once she was done cooking, she prepared herself to tell Rob that he would have to watch the baby. She had known last week that she would not have enough money for daycare, but she knew he would have flipped the script on her.

"Baby, come here," she said, slicing a piece of steak from the pan and picking it up with a fork. She blew it to cool it off.

"S'up, Pumpkin?' he said, calling her by the pet name he had given her when he wasn't calling her fat bitch.

"Here, taste this," she said, placing the food in his mouth. She waited to see what he would say. "Well? How is it?"

"I don't know; it kinda tastes like dog shit," he said, frowning up his face, and they both burst out in laughter

"Go to hell, Robert," she said, and turned around to begin fixing his plate.

He smacked her on the behind. "As long as you come with me, I'm all for it."

"Is Junior still sleeping?" Brandy asked, looking over her shoulder.

"Yep, and when he wakes up, he's going to drive them folks at the daycare crazy."

Ignoring his last comment about the daycare, she placed their food on the table. "Sit down and let's eat."

They took a seat at the table and talked about the problem Rob's mother was having with her health. "Make sure you tell her to check her sugar often. Four hundred is way too high, Rob. She could go into a diabetic coma."

"I know, right?" he replied. He got up and began to clear the table.

"I'm going to shower and get ready for work. Oh," she said spinning back around just before she walked out of the kitchen. "Junior has to stay here this week. He's not going to the daycare."

"Wait, what did you say?" Rob cocked his head to the side. "What the fuck for Brandy? He has a daycare. You'd better take his little crying ass there. Hell, you don't pay me to watch him; you pay them white folks to put up with all that crying and shit." Shaking his head, he began to speak more to himself than to her. "I have some shit to do anyway. This ain't overtime for you. This is your regular shift, any damn way. I don't get shit out of the deal. Naw, I'm not cool with that."

Getting pissed at him, she couldn't believe that he would talk like that about watching his own son. "This is your f'in son, too, Rob. You're supposed to watch him when I can't pay daycare. We talked about this before, and every time this time comes around, you start complaining."

"Who do you think watches him when you take your fat ass to the store, out clubbing, or even when you work overtime? Me! So don't sit here and act like I don't do my share," he said, walking up in her face. "Where in fuck is the money anyway, Brandy? All this overtime you're doing, and you don't have a damn thing to show for it. What, you spending it on some other nigga at the hospital? You cheating on me, Brandy?"

This time Brandy decided to take a different approach because she didn't want to fight. "No, honey, I'm not cheating, but you know I had to pay the car note and the rent out of this week's check, on top of the things that I buy for you. Then the money I had in the top drawer in my room is missing. I—"

Wham! Before she could complete her sentence, he had knocked fire from her. "Are you trying to say that you buy shit for me, huh? Are you trying to say you take care me, like I ain't a man? Or, better yet, are you trying to say that I stole the money?" Spit flew out of his mouth. He was so mad, not because she had accused him, but, deep down inside, because he knew he had taken it, and she was taking care of him, too. Not wanting to beat her too badly, but wanting to make himself feel better by giving her pain, he took her arm and twisted to where it felt as if it was going to break.

"Ouch, please stop, Rob. I'm sorry; it's not your fault. I overspent this week. I'm sorry," she cried.

"And what about the money?" he applied a little more pressure on her arm.

"I spent it or misplaced it. Rob, I'm sorry; please let me go. I need to go to work. Please."

"I don't want to ever hear you speak like that again. You hear me?" He let her arm go.

"Yes," she said, crying and shaking her head. Brandy began to massage her arm.

"Now since you had this already planned without asking me, I'm going to tell you how it's going to work out. You are going to leave me some money on that damn counter before you leave, just like you do at the daycare. Understood?"

"Yes."

"Yes, what?"

"Yes, king."

Brandy rolled her eyes as Rob walked out of the kitchen. Before getting ready for work, Brandy made sure she placed her last fifty dollars on the kitchen counter just as Rob had said.

Chapter Nine

Von

"Money talks and bullshit walks. For the right price, niggas would sell their fucking momma out. Niggas would have their own daughters on the streets, selling ass just to make a dollar. Nigga, you know that." Von looked over to his right at his cousin Travis, who was sitting in the passenger seat of his Excursion. They were in the parking lot of a shopping center—across the street from where Jay had been shot—waiting on a nigga who they had been told would have some info on who shot his brother.

Travis looked over at Von. "You're right about that, but I just hope this bitch ain't lying, and ain't been paid to try to set us up." Travis was referring to the girl who worked at Wing Stop.

Von had been all up and down Crenshaw Blvd., trying to find out who the niggas were, or what hood they were from, who had shot his brother. So far, he'd come up with nothing. He'd hit up two of the hoods in the area, but niggas weren't talking. This right here, talking to ole boy, was the last route he would take before he and his goons started shooting up any and everybody. If innocent people had to die, then it was what it was. He was going to avenge his brother at any expense. Von could have had his goons handle it themselves or even paid some other niggas to do it, but the shit was doubly personal. They had put his brother in a coma, thinking that it was him.

Von and Travis watched as a brown-skinned dude with dreads and a black duffle bag on his shoulder rolled up on a bike. It was like eighty-five degrees outside, and dude was dressed in all black. Von looked at his watch, "Just like she said, the nigga would be here at noon."

"Ain't that a fucking coincidence? The bitch knew exactly what time he was coming up here. I understand that this DVD shit is his hustle, but ain't no way a black mofo is showing up to work on time, especially at his own place of business."

Von didn't say a word. He was use to Travis' over-paranoid ass. He appreciated it, though; a few times his paranoia had saved their lives, and taken the life of the nigga who was trying to body them. Von pressed 'talk' on his cell phone, put it on speaker, and while it rang, he looked at Travis, who had his eyes glued on dude.

"S'up, Von?" a deep baritone voice blared through the phone.

"Alright, that's the nigga right here on the bike. I'm about to get out."

"We got you, dog," said the goon. Then you heard several guns being cocked.

Travis cracked a smile at how Von was two steps ahead of him. Without any notice, Travis hopped out the truck. Von didn't even end the call; he just jumped out behind him.

"What's up, homie. Let me holla at you," Travis said to dude as he was walking up on him.

"You're Mike, right?" Von asked as he stared the nigga dead in his eyes.

"Yeah, what's up? Y'all want some DVD's," dude asked, knowing that the way these two niggas were looking, bootleg DVD's were far from their mind.

Von went in his pocket, and pulled out a rubber-banded stack of hundreds. He looked at Travis and gave him a head nod. Travis walked over and removed the duffle bag from around dude's neck. Von tossed him the stack of money, which he didn't hesitate to catch.

"Come take a ride with us," Von told him.

Travis didn't wait for a reply; he grabbed Mike by the arm and said, "Let's go."

"Look, y'all, I appreciate y'all buying my movies, but why I gotta leave with y'all?" he said nervously.

"A few weeks back, a nigga was gunned down in front of Wing Stop. He was driving a red Ashton. That was my brother, my identical-twin brother. I heard you know what happened."

Dude immediately regretted having run his mouth. He didn't know who had ratted him out: the other niggas who hung up there with him; the people who worked in Wing Stop; or, the drunks who sat in front of the hamburger stand. He swallowed the lump in his throat and dropped his bike. As he was being pulled to the car by Travis, he asked, "Will I ever get a chance to spend this money?"

Von shrugged his shoulders. It was up to Travis, but knowing Travis' paranoid ass, he would probably want to off him, thinking that he would sing to the police. Although he didn't want to, Mike got into the backseat of the truck, praying that the niggas who'd just blessed him with the most money he'd ever had, would also spare his life so he could spend it.

A few miles down Crenshaw, less than ten minutes from where they'd picked up Mike, they pulled behind the Crenshaw Mall, into the parking lot of an abandoned retail chain. When Mike saw where they had taken him, he began to regret not putting up a fight. He knew that, eventually, running his mouth was going to get him in trouble; he just wished it had been another time and a different kind of punishment than what he was sure he was going to get.

Von killed the engine on the truck, and Travis opened up the rear, driver's side door. When he looked at Mike, he was sweating profusely, and it looked as if his brown skin had turned pale. But Travis had no pity for him; he hated niggas who ran their mouths.

"Get out the car," Travis ordered. Mike slowly eased his way out of the vehicle.

Von signaled his niggas who were following to take their positions. Once the three goons made their way out the car and posted in front of the building, Von made his way inside the retail store. Travis and Mike were right behind him.

"Have a seat right there," Travis pointed in the middle of the floor.

Mike looked around, and since the entire store was empty except for the dust and a little trash on the floor, he felt a little relived. Like in the movies, he was expecting to see a chair, rope, and chains. Mike took a seat and crossed his leg.

"I need to know the same story that you've been going around telling about who shot the nigga in the Ashton."

Von added, "Leave out all the extras. Tell me where you were standing, what you saw, and what you heard."

Mike directed his attention on Von. "First, I want to say that, if I had known that you or anybody else wanted to know what went down, I would have told y'all. Judging by the car, I thought it was just some rich brother who ended up in the wrong area and got . . . got—" Mike swallowed his words when shots from the outside began to sound off.

Boc boc boc It sounded like thunder. Travis aimed his pistol on Mike, and Von quickly pulled out his.

"It's a setup," one of the goons on the outside yelled.

"I didn't have anything to do with it." Mike covered his face. Seeing the look in Travis' eyes, he knew for sure that he was about to let him have it.

"Who shot—"

Before Von could finish his question, Travis had shot Mike in the stomach. He instantly removed his hands from his face and grabbed his stomach.

"That's fucked up," he cried in pain. "I ain't telling you niggas shit. YOU FUCKING SHOT MEEEEEE—"

Travis silenced him with one to the head.

In the meantime, the shots outside were still going off. Von and Travis ran to the door. There was a black van and a blue pickup truck going down the street, both with two dudes hanging out the windows shooting. All of their goons were in the middle of the street, shooting at the vehicles.

"Let's go. One-time's about to be here in no time," Travis hollered to Von.

He was right. They were in the outskirts of the Jungle, one of the most dangerous neighborhoods in Los Angeles. The way the movie *Training Day* portrayed the neighborhood was only half of how it really was. Best believe, an army of police was on the way, and they would gun down every last one of their black asses.

Von and Travis hopped in the truck. They pulled to the end of the parking lot, and Travis yelled, "Come on. Let's go." The three goons were already headed back that way. Von punched out of the driveway.

"Fuck, we still ain't got no fucking leads." Von hit the steering wheel. He made his way down Stocker and took the back streets all the way to the freeway entrance on Slauson.

CRSO

Two Weeks Later . . .

Brandy

Brandy stepped out of her 2004 Honda Accord in the parking garage of the hospital and slammed her door. Looking around at all of the newer-model vehicles only intensified her anger. She threw her purse over her shoulder and speed-walked up to the double doors of the hospital.

"Everyone and their mammy has a new car and home, but I can't see the light. No, fuck the light, I can't even afford to pay for the damn daycare," she mumbled under her breath. Needing to calm down a few notches, she decided to take the long route to ICU. "How will I ever get ahead? The bills are piling up, and Rob hasn't made this situation any easier for me. I had to pay him for the last two damn weeks to watch Junior," she continued mumbling.

She shook her head as she rounded the corner, passing up the gift shop. She looked to her left at the sign for the ladies' room. "Fuck that! I'm not stopping in there to make sure these bruises are covered this time. If anyone sees them, then maybe they will encourage me enough to leave that son of a bitch."

"Excuse me? Did you say something?" an elderly woman who was standing by the elevator asked her.

Not realizing that she had spoken aloud, Brandy shook her head and stepped on the elevator. She pressed the button for the fourth floor. The elderly woman stepped on right behind her. Brandy felt her staring at her, so she turned and looked at her. "Is there a problem?"

"No, I'm just fine but, since you asked, I was wondering are you o.k., darling. The side of your neck looks a little blue."

Wishing she had worn a turtleneck under her uniform, Brandy felt uncomfortable and decided to stop in the nearest restroom to put on her makeup. "I'm just fine," she replied, stepping off the elevators. As the door started to close, she heard the old woman say, "Humph! I'll bet you are."

CR80

After she had finished covering up her bruises, she left out the restroom and got the report from the nurse who was leaving morning shift.

"Hello, Mr. JayVon Deeds. It's me, again, Brandy Carter, and I will be your nurse for today." She continued to speak to Jay as if he could hear her. At the same time, she was checking his vitals and preparing to change his feeding tube. "As of today, you have been here a month and a half. Today is April first, two thousand thirteen. Right now, I'm hooking up your bag so that you will have your fluids. We want to make sure that you don't get dehydrated."

She plugged the tube into his IV, then placed the bag on the hook above his head. Since she worked in ICU, she was one-on-one with Jay, and working with him everyday caused her to look forward to seeing him. Maybe because he couldn't talk back, she could be herself and share her deepest secrets, or maybe because he's Von's twin brother. Even though Von was her friend's baby-daddy, she secretly had a crush on him. On many occasions, she had thought to step to him, but whenever he came around, she was nervous, and her tongue got stuck in her throat. Brandy smiled and looked down on him.

"I don't know, Mr. Deeds, but whatever it is, I know that I am beginning to feel a connection. Maybe it's a sign that, one day, I'll be your sister-in-law." She laughed at her own joke, but really wished that it would come true. "Yeah, wouldn't that be the day!" Her smile widened at the thought of her being Mrs. TrayVon Deeds.

"He only has one brother, so how would you become his sister-in-law?"

Brandy's heart dropped when she heard the deep voice behind her. She was so embarrassed that Von had overheard her talking to his brother, and obviously about him. She turned around with a nervous smile and stared at him. Von eyed her curvaceous body and licked his lips.

"So tell me what's on your mind, baby girl?"

Von was all for hitting it. If she didn't care that she and Coco were cool, neither did he. A bitch would be just that—a bitch—but he would always be her baby-daddy, which meant if Coco was to ever find out, she would forgive him.

"Hmmm. What's up with you?" Brandy looked down at the floor.

Von was ready to make a proposition, but his phone went off, letting him know that he had a text. As he read the text from Travis, his blood pressure began to rise. He looked up at Brandy. "I'll be back. I need to go take this call. Just in case you aren't here when I get back, I give you permission to use my number—for personal reasons." He winked and left out. He wanted to hurry up and find out what the fuck was going on with Coco.

I sure will use your number. This time she thought it to herself. Today is turning out alright.

After Von left, Brandy gave JayVon her undivided attention. "You're at peace. I can tell. Do you really want to come back to this cruel world? Sometimes I wish I was where you are, without any worries, stress, or pain. You're probably enjoying yourself, huh? I bet you are. I would, too, but since the Lord isn't ready for me, and my son needs me, I will make the best of my stay here. I will start by making Brandy feel superior from now on."

Brandy walked over to the sink and grabbed a face towel, shaving cream, and razor, then walked back over to JayVon's bedside.

"Mr. Deeds, I'm going to sit you up just a little so I can shave you. It doesn't look like anyone has shaved you in a few days. Your hair is growing all over the place. Hmmm, I wonder where your wife is. I haven't seen her in weeks. I hope she's o.k. You know I had to call your brother to come and get her one day. She was so down. She looked like she hadn't had any rest since you were admitted here."

She picked the shaving cream, squirted some in her hands, and rubbed it on both sides of his face. "You know you have nice skin, Mr. Deeds. You're a very handsome man. Do you like your women submissive?"

Brandy began to think about her situation at home, and how she had to submit to her baby-daddy's every need, only to be verbally and physically abused. Her thoughts caused her eyes to water and a burning sensation in her throat.

"Can I ask you something? I wonder if you're faithful. Are you faithful? Do you love your wife? Does she ever make you mad enough to smack her?" She lifted the razor to his face and slowly began to shave him as she continued to carry on a one-way conversation. "Naw, you don't hit her. You don't look like the kind of man who would put your hands on a woman. I saw your wife. She's beautiful. Seeing her stay by your side when you first arrived here, crying her poor heart out, I felt so bad for her. That said a lot about you. There is no way you could be beating on her; nope, not if she stayed by your side like that. I could see the love she has for you just by the way she looked at you. Yeah, I bet you're a good man. Now, your brother, I don't know. I do know a little something about him. He seems different from you, though."

She took the razor, put it in the water to rinse it out, and began to shave the other side. "Can I tell you a secret?" she whispered. "My son's father beats me every week. It doesn't matter what I do; nothing is ever good enough. He calls me names, and get this: He makes me pay him to watch our own son. Yeah, I know that's crazy, right? Would you every do that? Nah, I don't believe you would. I don't think I told you, but I have a little, chunky, three-year-old boy." Brandy felt herself getting excited just thinking about her baby. "He brings me so much joy. I love him so much. I can't find him a good father. Yep, I said find, because who would want me?"

Tap tap

Brandy turned around to see another nurse standing by the door. "Brandy, can you give me a hand when you're done?" the nurse asked.

"Sure, give me just a minute," she said.

The nurse closed the door, wondering why in the hell she always talking to him. Not sure how much she'd heard, Brandy decided to be quiet, but a song that her mother use to sing to her when she was feeling down came to mind, and before she knew it, she was softly singing and finishing up his shave.

Though the storms keep on raging in my life
And sometimes it's hard to tell the night from day
Still that hope that lies within is reassured as I keep my eyes upon the distant shore
I know He'll lead me safely to that blessed place He has prepared
But if the storms don't cease and if the winds keep on blowing in my life
My soul has been anchored in the Lord

Nivea

As Nivea came closer to her husband's room, she began to feel sick to her stomach. She had been beating herself up with guilt. After the night she'd spent with Von, she hadn't been able to look at herself. He'd called a few times, but she'd sent him straight to voicemail. She'd been trying her best to avoid him; but the more time passed, the more that night replayed in her mind, and the more she was tempted to call him back.

When she thought about how much damage she had already caused, and what could happen if she kept it up, she would hang up the phone. *Nivea, this isn't you, girl. Get it together. Think about your husband, for Christ's sake.* After tossing and turning, she would finally fall asleep with a pillow between her legs.

Okay, Niv, take a deep breath and open the door. He isn't even awake yet. He can only read you when he stares deep into your eyes, her inner voice said.

She felt like a little girl who had done something wrong and was about to face her father. Taking a deep breath, she placed her hands on the knob, slowly turning and pushing it open. All the butterflies in her stomach instantly stopped when she saw the nurse running her hands down the side of her husband's face and singing a song, *I am anchored in the Lord.*

"Umm umm," she cleared her throat, getting Brandy's attention.

"Ah . . . oh . . . hellllo," she stuttered, surprised to see his wife standing there. "You're right on time. I just finished shaving him, and I was rubbing my hands on the side of his face to see if I missed any hairs."

Nivea gave Brandy a once-over and compared her Asian and black, five-foot-four, one-hundred-ten pounds to Brandy's tall, big self, and knew for sure that she would never have a chance with her husband; but, so what? She still didn't want her shaving what belonged to her.

"Thank you, but I'm here now, and I'll finish that. From here on out, I'll shave my own husband."

"No problem. I'll put that on his charts. If you can give me a few minutes, I'll be back to update you on him. I've gotta go help another nurse," Brandy said, feeling embarrassed as she walked out the door, leaving Nivea and JayVon alone.

Nivea sat on the side of the bed for five long minutes, lost in her thoughts and feeling numb. She almost didn't want to look at him, afraid that he would wake up and find her out. The man who lay in the bed—her husband, her heart, and her better half—the man who she would, on a normal day, talk his head off, she had no words for at all today. Finally, looking at him, flashbacks of her rendezvous with Von crossed her mind. She stood up to leave, thinking she wasn't ready to face him yet, even in a coma.

Before she could take a step, in walked Von. He stood there, burning a hole through her with his eyes. She hated when her husband did that, and now Von was doing the same thing. It made her uncomfortable. She didn't want to let him in on her thoughts; but right on cue, as if she had opened her mouth, Von was right up on her, in her personal space. Nivea begin to shake her head no, but Von pressed his lips against hers and backed her up against the window, allowing his tongue to attack hers.

She never really had a chance to resist nor did she want to. Nivea's heart was beating fast and her clit was throbbing for Von's touch. Von turned her around and placed her hands up above her head, palms flat against the window, in a frisk-me position. He cockily placed his hands behind his back and pressed his body against her ass so that his dick could speak to her as he moved in a circular motion while it grew long and hard.

Nivea wanted him bad. She didn't give a care if anyone walked in or, even at the moment, if her husband woke up. Her mind was dick-blinded. The friction she felt from her clit pressed hard up against the windowsill, and Von's huge penis growing as he rotated his hips, had her moaning.

Wanting to turn the heat on her, Von finally brought his hand around to the front, and slid it down her pants to feel how wet she was. He didn't have to move his fingers around; he just stuck them deep up in her as she went crazy trying to ride them. Light moans began to escape her mouth and her breathing was heavy. She was nearing her nut and was about to go crazy; but, just like that, Von stopped. He removed his hand, pushed her hair to the left side of her neck, leaned in close so his lips barely touched her neck, and said, "It's wet just for me. When you stop playing games, you know how to find me." Then he walked out the room, leaving her standing there, out of breath and speechless.

Dammit! Nivea thought. She was pissed off. How could he come in and attack her like that? Get her all hot, then leave her cold? She dropped her head low at the thought of what had just happened in her husband's presence and knowing where she was headed once she left his room. She walked over to the side of the bed, bent down, kissed his cheek, and whispered in his ear, "Baby I'm sorry." She left without getting the update from the nurse about her husband's progress.

CR80

Across Town . . .

Coco and Brandy

Coco sat at the bar of The Game Sports Bar, sipping on her second round of rum-and-coke. It had her a little relaxed. She was still in a funk because Von had been giving her the cold shoulder every since she'd gone over to Nivea's house, showing her ass. The one time he had come home was just to check on their son and bring him toys that he didn't need, while he ignored the hell out of her in the process.

She was tired of his bullshit and had decided to step out tonight. Looking around the dimly-lit club, she noticed a few niggas she'd messed with in the past, but nothing major. After realizing their money wasn't long enough, she'd dumped them. In her mind, she wasn't exactly what you'd call a gold digger; but, "Why fuck with a broke nigga," was her motto.

As she picked up her phone to call Brandy for the third time in an hour, Brandy eased up behind her, took the phone out of her hand, and put it back in her purse.

"Damn, bitch, it took you long enough! What the hell happened this time? That lazy nigga made you rub his feet or some shit?"

"Look, I don't want to talk about his ass," Brandy replied, looking around the club. "I just left work and I had to get dressed at my co-worker's crib. Anyway, it looks like some ballers are in the house tonight."

Coco frowned upon hearing Brandy sounding stupid, but then changed her facial expression when she responded. "Yeah, it's a little money up in here." On the inside, she was thinking, *How in hell does she know what a baller looks like with a scrub at home? Please.* "Your hair looks cute," she said, changing the subject because she didn't want to talk about ballers with her.

"Oh yeah, you like it?" Brandy touched it to make sure her short, lace-front bob was still intact. When the bartender walked over, Brandy said, "I want what she's drinking," with a big Kool-Aid smile on her face.

"Make that another round of rum-and-coke for me, too. It's about to be a long night if she's happy," Coco added.

After the women got their drinks, Coco thought, *I might as well ask her what the hell she's smiling about,* even though she really didn't care to know. "Spill the beans. What are you smiling about?"

"I thought you'd never ask. Anyway, I met someone."

Oh boy, here we go, Coco thought, rolling her eyes in her head. "Where? At the meat market, bussing dishes?" Coco laughed.

"No, and that's why I don't tell you shit. You've always got jokes, Coco. Everyone can't snag two ballers," she said, referring to Coco messing with Von and Dre. Brandy hated how Coco was always clowning her or acting as if she was beneath her. What Coco didn't realize was that, every time she drank, her true feelings came out, but that only helped push Brandy to further pursue her prey—Von! *Why you're acting like your shit is all good, your nigga is willing to give me some of that good-good you're always bragging about.*

"Girl, you know I'm joking. Don't mind me." She stopped when she heard her song and threw her hands up, "Ayyyye! That's my jammmm! Come on, girl, we came to have some fun tonight. Let's hit the dance floor." She took hold of Brandy's hand and pulled her out to the dance floor with her. "You know I can't sit on this song," Coco yelled over the loud music. Once she stepped foot on the dance floor, Brandy stepped to the side to sip a little more, while Coco did her thing to Trey Songz' *Panty Dropper.*

CR80

Dre was leaned back, with one leg up on the wall, in his D-boy stand, staring at Coco as she moved her hips on the dance floor. He was still salty that she'd left him that night when they were chilling because he was talking about her baby-daddy's brother. He knew she was bad for him; countless times, he'd told himself that he was going to quit fuckin' with her, since she only ran to him when that soft-ass nigga wasn't treating her right. *But, damn!* he thought, seeing her in the short, gray-and-light-blue, shoulderless dress with the sides cut out, looking as if it had been painted on her to make her curves stand out more. As bad as he wanted to go snatch her up, he didn't. He did not want to come off as soft, so he chilled but kept an eye on her, making sure no other nigga tried to push up on her.

The DJ switched the song up and was now playing *Fall for Your Type,* by Jamie Foxx featuring Drake. Coco saw Dre posted up, with his hat low to his eyes, red Polo shirt, creased-up jeans slightly baggy, with his Polo boots and the iced-out watch, looking hella thugalicious. She wanted him to scoop her up and duck off in some corner, but she didn't want to approach him first, so she put an extra twirl into her motion, thinking he would make a move.

She knew the control she had over him; he could never stop messing with her. To her surprise, he was still standing there, trying to ignore her like he didn't see her in that come-freak-me dress that Von never would have allowed her to step out of the house in. Since the DJ was now playing the song he'd dedicated to her, and on different occasions he would spit a few bars to her while she sat back admiring his skills, she decided to walk over to him.

Fuck it. Von wants to be on some silent-treatment shit, I'm feeling too good to sleep alone tonight, Coco thought as she did her best *Top Model* strut his way. Dre knew what time it was. He was glad this time he hadn't moved when he'd wanted to. This time she gave in. He watched her walking over to him in her six-inch pumps. He began to mouth the lyrics to the song:

Can I, can I save you from you
'Cause you know there's something missing
And that champagne you've been sipping
I suppose to make you different all the time
Is starting to feel like the wrong thing to do, girl
'Cause with all that recognition
It gets hard for you to listen to the things
That I must say to make you mine
But live girl, have some fun, girl
We'll be fine
Trying to convince myself I've found one
Making the mistake I never learned from

I swear I always fall for your type, yeah

For your type

Tell me why I always fall for your type

For your type

(I just can't explain this shit at all)

Fall for your type

(I just can't explain this shit at all)

Fall for your type

I can't understand why she still wants to be with fuck-a-nigga, but I'mma take care of that and soon, he thought, licking his lips and bouncing his head to the beat, now holding tight onto Coco's hips, as she was grinding up on him.

Brandy went back to the bar for another drink. She wanted to have fun, too, but Coco's words cut deep, so she sipped her drink and watched Coco dry-fuck Dre on the dance floor as if she didn't have a care in the world. *Hmmm, she needs to choose one before I do it for her!* she thought, thinking about what had taken place earlier that day. When she thought about Von telling her to call him, her spirits were lifted. She began smiling from ear-to-ear.

"S'up sexy? You want to dance?" some random guy asked. "Sure," she said, still smiling and thinking about how she was finally getting a chance to hook-up with Von. The guy took Brandy by the hand, and they went and found a spot on the dance floor.

"Come on, girl, let's go chill. You're trying to get me worked up in here so you go run home to that cat." Dre was all in Coco's ear. He wanted to know upfront what was up.

"Fuck him, Dre, I'm with you tonight. So chill. Don't bring him up." She lifted her head and pecked him on the lips. Any other time, messing with Dre in public was off limits, but tonight she was doing her. "Let's leave now, Dre." She was getting hot and bothered.

"Naw, we can chill in VIP for a cool second. I'm waiting to holla at someone," he explained.

Coco pouted but she understood his "lil" hustle. "Oh damn, where's my girl," she said aloud when she realized she had forgotten about Brandy.

"She's on the floor with my homeboy; she's straight." Dre nodded his head in her direction. Suddenly Dre's cool demeanor turned hot, and he was mean-mugging the nigga walking his way.

$$\text{CR}\mathcal{EO}$$

Von and Coco

Von pulled up to the club, tucked his heat in his waist, and hopped out of his new Ashton, leaving the keys in the ignition and the engine running. He nodded his head at the valet and kept it moving. They knew that the head nod simply meant, 'Do not move my car, and have it ready for me to burn out.'

Getting the call from Travis that Coco was up in his spot, where he was well-known, hugged up with his enemy, had him tight. Although the love the wasn't there he still had to see for himself.

"S'up, Bruce?" He gave the bouncer at the entrance dap.

"I can't call it, baby. VIP all day," Bruce said, letting him know where Coco was.

"A'ight." Von walked through the doors, headed straight for VIP.

Brandy saw Von as soon as he walked in, and the way he looked, screamed, "No nonsense, confident, money, and fine as hell." Making eye contact with him for just those few seconds, she threw her hands up in the air, winding her body to the floor, hoping he would get a good glimpse of her in her all-over body suit.

Damn! Von thought, then turned his head and brought his mind back to why he was there. Walking straight up to their table, Von smirked at Dre's mean-mug.

"S'up Co? So this is how you do it now?" he said, staring at Dre.

Coco didn't know how long he'd been in the club, but she was no fool. She was going to deny it all. "Do what, Von? You know we grew up together. We were just chilling," she said, standing up.

"Man, Co, sit back down. You ain't got to explain shit to him." Dre stood to his feet.

Biting on the inside of his jaw, Von thought about his next move. "Nigga, this is my bitch," he said, poking Coco on the shoulder. "I tell this bitch what to do. Fuck nigga, you ain't learned from the last time that I am a boss?"

"Von, how the hell you gonna come in here accusing me, when you've had your ass out for the last two weeks? Who you fucking with, Von? Why in the hell I ain't seen you? Where you been?" Coco thought about how he hadn't been paying her any attention, but wanted to talk shit and check who she was with.

Hearing Coco go off about her nigga not coming home touched Dre's heart—and the cold part about it was he'd been called out on it in public. But he knew the bitch was using him— again. *That bitch is going to pay; fuck how I feel about her.* Dre played it off like he wasn't tripping off Coco and got back at Von.

"Naw, I didn't catch the lesson. How about you run it back by me again," Dre said, pissed off that Von was still breathing.

Von and Dre were inches away from each other. Dre could smell the mint on Von's breath, and Von could smell the alcohol on Dre's.

"Yo, my nigga, check it. Unlike you, I don't give lessons over washed-up pussy. But I'm going to do you a favor this time; I'mma spare you," Von spat.

"Yeah, fuck-boy, you do that," he said to Von's back as he walked off. "You been sparing a lot of lives I hear. Nigga talking about he's a boss, but he can't even find out who was out to body him. Nigga's weak."

Von shot back around, ready to knock his ass out, but security grabbed him. "He ain't worth it, man. Get at him another time; too many witnesses."

"Fuck, that nigga ain't about it. Let him go." Dre braked.

Dre was getting all rowdy in front of the crowd that had formed around them. "He's supposedly got the streets scared, but me? Shit, one thing about me, I never miss my target," he said, putting up his hands in a shape of a gun, as if he was shooting at Von.

That was all it took for Von to break loose from security's grip. Before you knew it, he had slammed Dre on the table, causing it to break and all the bottles of Patron to hit the floor. Dre was no match for Von. Von also had one up on him because Dre had been drinking. Von started raining blows. Dre's homies came running, pushing through the crowd, but were stopped in their tracks when gunshots were fired in the air. Travis had seen them coming and wasted no time putting a stop to them.

Von pulled his piece from his back, and put it in Dre's face. "Talk that shit now! I don't hear you, fuck-boy."

Von was zoned-out, not even knowing what was going on around him. Coco was screaming, and begging Von to leave the club. She didn't want Von to shoot Dre. One, Dre was her friend; and two, Von might go to jail forever. "No, Von baby, let him go. Let's get out of here, baby." She grabbed his arm.

"Let's roll out man; the po-po is about to shake the spot," Travis yelled, finally breaking Von out of his zone.

Von yanked his arm away from Coco and removed the gun from Dre's face "This is the last lesson, fuck-boy. Playtime is over, just like it was for your DVD man," he smirked, talking about Dre's little homie who Travis had killed in the abandoned building. Von got off Dre and ran out of the club, with Travis in tow.

Chapter Ten

Nivea

When Nivea left the hospital after her visit with her husband, her mind was made up. She couldn't fight the craving any longer, and leaving her husband's bedside only proved that, after *one dose* of Von, she was hooked.

How can I be so cold-hearted? One minute hating to see him coming; the next minute craving his touch? She questioned herself. *Hmmm, I'll bet this is how every woman feels who gets caught up in him,* she thought. *I can't really place the blame on him. I was the one who pushed up on him first, but he could have tried resisting me more. The question is, 'Would I have let him?' Hell no! I needed him that night, and by the looks if it, he needed me as well,* she thought, answering herself, trying to make excuses for her infidelity. As she drove along the highway, allowing the breeze to caress her skin, she tried reversing her train of thought. *This is it. There's no point in battling with this anymore. I can't undo what's been done. If Jay wakes up, I'll just—*

Brrrr brrrr

Before she had a chance to finish her thought, her phone started ringing. Thinking it might be Von, she snatched it up quickly from the passenger seat, not even looking at the number.

"Hello," she answered, trying not to sound excited.

"Hey, Chunky," her cousin Allie said, sounding all cheerful, calling her by a nickname she hated.

She rolled her eyes because she really wasn't in the mood to talk to anyone else right about now. She was on a mission; one that was filled with lust.

"Hi, Allie, what's been going on with you?"

"Well, you sure sound dry! I'm happy to hear from you, too."

Now feeling bad that her favorite cousin had detected her mood, she decided to apologize and changed her tone. "I'm sorry, Lei-Lei, I've been going through a lot since the last time I spoke with you. I've been under a lot of stress. So much has happened over the past two months, I'm confused and lost, Lei," she said, feeling the tension building back up and the stress overwhelming her once again.

"Awww, Chunky, I'm sorry to hear that. What could possibly be going on so bad in your life that would have you stressed and sounding like your world is crumbling down? No, wait, we can talk about that later. Right now, I may have some good news that would cause you to feel much better."

"What is it?" she said, knowing no amount of good news could make her feel better about her secret. *But, hey, if she wanted to try, then why not let her give it a shot?*

"O.k., if your dad hasn't told you yet, which I have a feeling he hasn't, I passed my classes this semester. And, I've been thinking about coming back home and going to USC, so that I can be closer to the family."

"Oh really, Allie? That's wonderful! I miss you like crazy. When will you be here?"

Hearing that her favorite cousin was coming home brought Nivea joy. It had been three years since she'd left California and moved to Tampa with her boyfriend while attending USF. Nivea had hated to see her leave, but she had known it was best for her. They had hung tight almost every day growing up; when you saw one, you would see the other. They were more like best friends and had even had a few catfights before. One thing Nivea loved about her was that she didn't mind telling her when she was wrong, but she always had her back.

"Well, what if I were to tell you that I'm standing at your front door, but I don't see your car, and if you don't get her in the next five minutes, I'm going back to Tampa—"

"You've got to be kidding me, right, Allie?" Nivea screamed with excitement. "Where the hell are you? I'm two minutes away from home."

"Well, you'd better get here," she said, then hung up the phone.

Nivea made it home in exactly three minutes. As soon as she parked her car, she jumped out and ran into her cousin's waiting arms. "I'm surprised you're here." She squeezed her for dear life! "Are you really moving back home? Is today your first day back? Where is Jack? Is he here with you?" she asked all in one breath, looking around for Allie's long-time boyfriend.

Allie began to laugh and shake her head. "Girl, can I get a glass of water and a nice soft couch to sit on, or do I have to stand out here in these six-inch heels to answer your questions?"

"Oh, excuse my manners. Yes, come in."

As soon as they walked in the family room, Nivea's mood changed. She couldn't help thinking of Von when she should be thinking of her husband.

Allie had always been the one to know when something wasn't right with her cousin. She asked, "Is everything okay, Chunky?"

"Oh my, yes, I'm okay. Let me get your water." Nivea tried to play it off.

"Naw, unh unh, honey." Allie placed one hand on her hip. "The way you sounded on the phone and the look on your face tells me that you'd better get me something stronger than water!"

Nivea went over to the bar, and fixed her and Allie a drink. Her stomach was full of butterflies. She didn't want to tell her cousin about Von, but she was planning to tell her that she had cheated. She just hoped her cousin didn't dig deeper, make her tell whom it was that she had slept with, and that he had invaded her every thought—when it should be her husband, who was still fighting for his life.

"You seem to have put on a few pounds in the hips and butt since the last time I saw you, Chunky." Allie looked her cousin up and down.

"Yeah, I have, but I kind of like it," she lied, but she had realized she was packing on extra pounds. "So tell me where is Jack?" she said, changing the subject.

"Jack and I are done. I felt like life was passing me by, but I was stuck in Jack's world."

"I don't understand. Jack is all you've ever known. He was your soul mate."

"You're right! That's just it; he is all I've ever had, all I've ever known. I've never had a chance to experience life with anyone else because I felt like I was in his cave, and the only way out was to leave him and leave the state. I love him, but I want to at least test the waters while I'm still young and fly."

"Wow!" Nivea was shocked; she didn't ever think that Allie and Jack would break up. "How did he take it?"

"At first, it was hard for the both of us. Hell, I've known him since middle school. After agreeing to always be friends-with-benefits, unless one of us is in a serious relationship, he accepted it for what it is, and here I am. Now, enough about me. What's with you stressing out all about?"

Nivea threw the glass back, and allowed the Patron to burn her throat before speaking. "Jay was shot. He's in a coma, and I can't seem to get my head right." She began to cry.

"What! OMG, Chunky! Why didn't you call me? I could have been here for you," Allie said, getting up, grabbing a couple of tissues, and handing them to Nivea, while rubbing her back.

No longer able to hold it in, she blurted it all out. "Allie, I cheated. I cheated while my husband was fighting for his life and, to be honest with you, I enjoyed it. I'm on my way over to his place after I pack an overnight bag."

Now it was Allie's turn to look shocked, with her mouth wide open and one hand over her chest. "You did what, Nivea? And when? How did this all happen?"

Nivea told her cousin the story from beginning to end, leaving out who the person was whom she'd slept with. By now, both of them were in tears.

Chapter Eleven

Von and Nivea

Von lay stretched out in his king-size bed, sleeping like a king. After the wild night he'd had at the club, then to come home and put a whippin' on a stress-releasing and much-needed vagina, he was bound to sleep all day. The smell of breakfast and Folgers coffee filled his nostrils. Since he lived alone at this house, he thought he was dreaming, until he heard the footsteps coming up the stairs. Von slid his nine millimeter with the silencer on it out from under the pillows and aimed it towards the door under the covers.

"Von, sweetie, I made you breakfast," Nivea announced as she turned the corner stepping into his bedroom, then pausing at the look on his face. She was all too familiar with that look. She herself had been in shock, too, the first time she had awakened and saw him in her bedroom—naked! "Hey," she smiled, trying to break the ice, "are you o.k.?"

"Yeah, what's up? I'm cool," he said, sliding his piece back under the pillows, now remembering why he wasn't alone and changing his facial expression. "What's that?" He nodded towards the food tray in her hand, staring at her curves in his tank top and licking his lips.

"I might can't fry chicken, but I have some bacon, eggs, and toast, with strawberries and grapes on the side, and a cup of coffee. I hope you're hungry." Nivea walked over to his side of the bed and placed the tray in front of him. She then went around and climbed in on her side of the bed, "My husband loves breakfast in bed—" The words had slipped out her mouth before she even realized what she had said. Now they both sat quiet, in their own thoughts. Her stomach curled up in knots as she realized, once again, that she was sleeping with her husband's brother.

Von hated the fact that he'd betrayed his brother, but he also felt that, it was what it was. This was life and shit happened.

"Sorry, I didn't mean to bring that up. Sometimes I feel like you are taking his place and I find I'm treating you like—"

"Shhhh," he said as he set the tray from in front of him. He leaned over to where she was. "Can I have some more of that good-good?" he said as he climbed on top of her.

Nivea bit her bottom lip. Her mouth watered as she looked up into his eyes. She was more than ready to go another round. As Nivea reached for his manhood, she ignored her ringing cell. She knew it was no one but Allie calling that early in the morning, and she wasn't about to explain herself. She was ready for Von to take her down. She took his manhood, and rubbed it up and down her throbbing, wet clit.

Von turned her over. "I want you to ride it." He sat her on top of him. Von gripped her butt as she rode him nice and slow. "Fucccck, Nivea," He couldn't help calling out her name. He'd had some good sex, but Nivea was the best. Von's phone started ringing. He thought it was Coco calling again, because she had been calling and apologizing all night.

Nivea began to speed up her pace. She had him ready to bust, but Von wasn't ready. He flipped her over and began to feed her nice, long strokes.

"Yessss . . . ahhhh . . . yessss . . . Give it to me," Nivea pleaded.

Von's cell went off again. He reached over and grabbed it off the dresser. Nivea didn't complain because he continued to feed her just the way she liked it. Von couldn't wait to burst Coco's bubble. "Yeah," he answered, sounding as if he was both out of breath and in pleasure.

"Oh shit . . . oh shit, Von." Nivea couldn't help herself. Her climax was coming.

Nurse Charlene cleared her throat and acted as if she wasn't hearing what she knew she was hearing. "Yes, this is Charlene from the hospital. I have some great news," she said, sounding excited. "I'm calling to let you know that your brother is awake. Come when you can and would you please contact his wife."

Her voice was so loud on the phone that Nivea overheard what was said; however, the news came at the same time she was climaxing, and she couldn't control her cries. "Ohhhhhh . . . Von . . .Von," she cried.

Von lay the phone down; he, too, was seconds away from releasing his load. "Arrrrgggghhhh . . . shit . . . girl. Damn!"

Nurse Charlene looked at the phone in disbelief of what she was hearing and hung up. The busy sound coming from the phone snatched them both from their trance.

Von looked at Nivea. "My brother is awake," he said, still slightly out of breath. Nivea didn't reply.

Chapter Twelve

Brandy

Brandy looked up as she heard the doorknob shaking. "Is there anyone in here?" a voice called out from the other side of the door. "Yes, I'll be out in a second," she replied, with a slight strain in her voice.

She was hunched over the sink in pain. This time Rob had really put a beating on her. That night after she'd left the club tipsy, she'd driven straight home, not bothering to take off her clubbing clothes. The moment she'd stepped foot in the house at three o'clock in the morning, Rob had put the worst beating on her ever. He'd beat her for hours, kicking and smashing her head against the wall, accusing her of staying out late cheating.

She had wondered if it was going to be the final whipping that took her life; but when he noticed her going in and out of consciousness, he had stopped hitting her. She no longer had the will to live, and wished he had killed her that night. That beating had caused her to miss two weeks of work, a fractured rib, and a humongous knot on her forehead.

"Ouch! Ouch!" she squealed in pain. "Damn you, Robert," she mumbled as she stared at herself in the mirror. She was glad to have a few doctors as friends who would prescribe any medication she needed so she didn't have to go to the hospital. Though she really wasn't healed enough to go back to work, the bills were stacking up. Rob was driving around in her car every day, pretending to look for work, only to come home smelling like beer and marijuana. So she'd had to go back to work.

Brandy stood up as best as she could and grabbed the Vicodin out of her purse. She popped two of the pills and washed them down with half a bottle of water. She took a few more moments to pull herself together before heading out of the employee restroom. Just as she was walking out of restroom, Monica's *Why I Love You So Much* ringtone began to play on her cell phone. She reached in her bag and sent the call straight to voicemail. This was Rob's seventh call since she'd left the house, and every time she'd refused the call.

After retrieving her patient files from the nurses' station, Brandy made her way to the room of her first patient of the night. Halfway down the hall, Monica's ringtone began to play again, causing Brandy to get irritated. "Why in the hell does he keep calling me?" she griped as she walked into JayVon's room, straight to the window, where she answered Rob's call.

"What is it, Robert?" she whispered in a low, angry tone.

"Baby, I've been calling and calling."

"That's obvious; now what the hell do you want, because today I'm not in the mood for your bullshit."

"Baby, I'm sorry; you know I was drunk and I'm—"

"Going to stop drinking," she finished his sentence for him. "Yeah I know all about it!"

"Listen to me, Brandy," Rob said, with tears streaming down his face. Although it had been two weeks, he was still feeling bad. He had never beaten her that bad. "Brandy, this is coming from the heart. I don't know what comes over me, but I'm trying to work on controlling my anger. I'm really sorry. I know I fucked up this time and I—"

"And you what Rob, huh? You what?" she asked, getting more upset by the second. "Let me guess. You want to marry me, right?" Chuckling a little, she added, "When? Before or after you kill me? I could have died, and you're sorry is the best you can come up with? Yeah, you're right. You are a sorry, sorry-ass nigga. Tell me this. When are you actually wholeheartedly sorry? Before you beat me or after? No, I can do better than that. Let's see. This time was the last time; no, maybe last week or last year. Hell, *you say* you're sorry every time; but I can't figure out a time you actually were. You tell me because I don't understand; maybe you can help me figure out what the hell is wrong with you. I am not your fucking punching bag. I'm sick of you, Robert, and I'm going to leave you if you don't get your act together," she said, all in one breath. "I swear this to you. This is the last time that I ever in my life take you back, and I put that on my dead mother. If you ever lay a hand on me again, that's it; I'm done, and I will walk out."

"Baby, don't talk like that. I'm going to prove it to you. I love you too much. You're my heartbeat. I can't let you go. I can't live without you and my son in my life. I'm going to prove it to you, baby. You hear me? Let's work on us. Me and you, baby; fuck what the world says."

The more he talked, the more her heart melted, and she became angry with herself. She knew she wasn't going anywhere anytime soon, at least not before she tried to get him help. She'd never heard him cry and beg this much before, so she figured he must be serious this time.

"Look, Rob I gotta go." She hung up the phone, turning it off in the process.

"You should have never gone back after the first time," Jay said in a raspy voice, his eyes still closed.

Brandy eyes bulged out as she quickly turned and faced him with one hand over her heart. "Oh my . . . gosh . . . you . . . you're awake," she stuttered.

"Yeah, and I meant what I said."

"Um, o.k., right! Um, wow! I'll be right back," she said, rushing out the room to get the report from the other nurse. She wondered how long he had been awake.

Chapter Thirteen ~ Welcome Home

Jay and Nivea

A week had passed since JayVon had come out of the coma, and now the day had come that he would finally be going home. He couldn't wait to be in the comfort of his own home again with the love of his life—his wife. He appreciated the love that he'd received from those near and dear but, other than his brother, he didn't want any company. All he wanted was to soak in a hot bath, and get some love and affection from his wife. Then, in a few days, check on what had been going on a Deeds Realty.

Nivea was fine with that. The way she had been feeling, she wasn't up for any company anyway. She damn sure didn't want Von coming over, but how could she tell her husband that.

JayVon said his goodbyes to a few of the hospital staff and thanked them for everything. He was hoping to see Brandy before he left, but she hadn't been at work the last two days. Before leaving the hospital, he made a mental note to come back to the hospital or call to make sure that she was alright, since he knew about her situation at home.

"Take care of yourself, Mr. Deeds," Nurse Charlene said as she shut the car door.

"You do the same, and thank you for everything," JayVon said and reclined his seat. He quickly leaned back up and looked out of the window. "Hey, Charlene," he called after her.

With her hands still on the wheelchair, Charlene looked back over her shoulder at JayVon.

"Yes?"

"Tell Brandy I said to take care of herself." He gave the nurse a wink and she smiled.

"I sure will. Bye." She turned around and began pushing the wheelchair back into the hospital.

"I see someone has made a few friends," Nivea retorted.

"Awww . . . Is my baby feeling some kind of way because her handsome husband is a ladies' man?" Jay placed his hand on her leg and squeezed it. "Damn, Nivea." he said, looking down at his boy sticking up in his basketball shorts.

"What?" Nivea looked away from the road. Her eyes followed Jay's, and she cracked a halfway smile. "Good to know that your wife still turns you on," she said, looking back at the road.

"Always and forever," he replied, "and I can't wait until we get home so you can show me how much I still turn you on. Damn, I know my hot-hot is tight." He moved his hand to her center and began to rub it. "Is Daddy making her wet?"

"Yes," Nivea lied. The truth was that she missed her husband and wanted badly to show him how much; but every time she looked at him, she thought of Von and the things that he'd made her feel as recently as two days ago. She'd sworn to herself—and told Von, too—that, after the other night, she would never sleep with him again. She didn't believe that, but she damn sure was going to try.

"Ouch!" JayVon said, removing his hand from Nivea's crotch and placing it on his shoulder. He was having sharp pains again.

"Honey, are you alright?" She looked over at him.

"Yeah." He laid his head back on the seat and closed his eyes. *The niggas straight tried to take me out,* he thought as the incident replayed in his head.

"Baby, do you want to fill your prescription now?" Nivea asked.

"No, I don't need any medicine."

Jay didn't sound convincing, but Nivea didn't bother to debate with him about it. She would simply fill it later. She knew that her husband hated medication, but she also knew that he would need the pain meds more than he realized.

"Oh, wow," Nivea mumbled when she turned on her block and noticed several cars parked near her house. She'd told Allie that her hubby wasn't up for company. *She is so hardheaded,* thought Nivea. She looked over at Jay, who still had his head back and his eyes closed. Nivea became light-headed when she noticed Von's car parked in front of the house. She knew she would have to face him again sooner than later, but she had been hoping for never. "Honey, we're home."

Jay rose up and smiled. He then leaned over and kissed his wife. "I need a bath." He winked.

Well, you won't be getting it now. We have guests. Nivea smiled back. She decided not to inform her husband of their guests. She may as well let it be a surprise. Nivea turned the car off and ran to the other side to open Jay's door. He had already opened it and was slowly getting out.

"You got it, baby? I can help you." Nivea took him by the arm.

"I'm good."

Jay used all his strength to rise from the seat. She held his hand as he took the steps up the porch. Before opening the door, she took a deep breath. Jay then grabbed her and pulled her into his arms.

"I love you. I love you so much. Baby, I knew God had sent me my good thing the first day I laid eyes on your sexy ass. It's because of you that I made it. I couldn't leave you, Niv." He took his hand and stroked her check. "Besides my mother and grandmother . . ." He thought about telling her that they had come and invited him to a peaceful place, but he'd declined it for now. "Besides my mother and grandmother, I don't think another woman could capture my heart like you three have." By now, tears where falling from her eyes. Jay leaned in and kissed her deeply.

"Welcome home!" everyone screamed in unison when Nivea and Jay walked into the door.

"Awww. What y'all want?" Jay laughed. He really didn't want company, but seeing all of their faces made him feel good. He decided to enjoy the moment. He looked around, taking everything and everyone in. There was Allie, Nivea's cousin, still looking pretty as ever. She and Nivea could pass for twins, except one was darker than the other. There was his cousin Travis, looking like the rapper Nelly; his assistant Stephanie and her man;

a few other workers from Deeds; Ray Ray and his brothers; and Von.

When Von and Jay made eye contact, their smiles could light up two worlds. Von made his way to his brother and hugged him as tight as he could. "I'm sorry man," he buried his face on his shoulder.

Jay didn't say anything. Although it hurt his heart to finally realize that his brother was the reason he'd been shot, at that moment, it didn't matter.

Looking at her husband and his twin share so much love, Nivea was beginning to feel sick to her stomach. Without being noticed, she rushed up the stairs to the first bathroom, and let out her lunch over the toilet.

CR80

Coco

"I don't know what I am going to say about how I found out that Jay was home, but I'm going over there." Coco undid her scarf and began to brush her wrap down as she continued to talk to herself. "Von has to have another bitch, and whoever she is, he has gotta be serious about her."

Coco was becoming more angry as she thought about her baby-daddy and suppose-to-be man not coming home; it had been almost a month now. That was something new, and she knew he had to be with a chick. The shit he was talking when he had decided to take her call was bullshit. He wasn't that damn mad that she had been talking to Dre. That was just an excuse.

It took Coco about two hours to get her and the baby ready. She was now in her car heading to Jay and Nivea's house, when she caught a flat and had to pull off the freeway about a mile down, into a gas station parking lot. "Fuck!" she cursed, thinking that AAA would take a good while before they got to her, and she would miss the event. She was anxious. When she got out the car, a panhandler offered to change her tire for a few bucks.

"Not a problem," she told him, then opened her trunk so he could get the tire. It was hot as hell out, so Coco took the baby out of the car seat, and went and stood in the shade.

"Ain't that the bitch who started that shit with the homeboys?" Coco heard someone say. When she looked up, there were four girls walking her way. She immediately noticed one was Dre's niece.

"What's up, Coco," Dre's niece Kyra asked.

They were still walking her way. Coco looked over at the man changing her tire, who was still trying to get the flat off. *Slow-ass fuck,* she thought. Coco didn't reply. She knew those bitches were up to something.

"Awww . . . Can I see him," Kyra asked, as she reached her hands out for Little Von.

Coco didn't budge or say a word. She kept her eyes on each of the bitches in front of her.

"Coco, don't you need to tell my uncle something? This baby sure looks like family," Kyra said, staring hard at baby Von. The high cheekbones, curly hair, and light-brown eyes sure reminded her of her Uncle Dre and her aunt Alberta, Dre's mom.

Coco continued to stay quiet; she knew what the bitch was saying but she wasn't about to play into that shit.

"Bitch, I don't like you; I think you're a rat. I don't know why the homie was fucking with you in the first place," one of the girls said, and poked Coco in her forehead. That got her a reaction from her.

"Bitch, you'd better step the fuck up out my face. Talk that shit when I don't have my baby," Coco barked.

"Let me see my little cousin, and y'all handle that," Kyra said, grabbing the baby.

"Bitch, get back!" Coco snapped at Kyra.

Coco was blindsided. The hit to the side of her head caused her to stumble, and she let the baby go. Kyra was there to catch him. Coco swung on the girl who hit her, and then the other three jumped in.

CRSD

Jay, Nivea, and Von

Back at the house, everyone was sitting around chatting and having a nice time. Allie had cooked chicken spaghetti, fried chicken, chicken enchiladas, and a few appetizers. She had also made Jay his favorite desert—peach pie. Nivea was standing in the kitchen with her cup up to the ice machine. After throwing up several times, her mouth was dry. Although Allie had it smelling good in the house, she wouldn't dare put a bite in her mouth just to have it come back up.

"Hey, baby, are you alright?" Jay came up behind her.

Truth was Nivea felt like shit and wanted everyone to get out. Would she admit it? Of course not. "I'm fine, baby." She put a few ice chips in her mouth before turning around to face Jay.

Jay studied Nivea's face. "Are you coming down with something? What's the matter?" He pulled her close, and with the back of his hand, he touched her forehead. "You look pale and you're a little warm."

"I'm just tired; that's all."

"I'm about to kick our guests out. You go upstairs and lie down."

Nivea gave Jay a warm smile and nodded her head to agree. "O.k., let me steal a plate first," she said, pretending that was the reason she'd stayed behind. The real reason was that she felt too weak to walk.

Jay kissed her forehead, and turned to walk out to go inform his guests that the party was over. "Don't be in there messing with my wife. She doesn't feel good," Jay told Von as he walked toward the kitchen.

Nivea was on the verge of hyperventilating when she saw Von walk in. *Why in the hell is he coming near me, knowing that his brother—my husband—is near?*

Von threw his hands up in surrender. "I'm making me a plate, that's all."

"Yeah, alright," Jay replied. "I'm about to send them home so Niv and I can chill." Jay continued to the living room.

"So y'all can chill, huh?" Von's sarcasm caused Nivea to roll her eyes in the top of her head.

"Don't hate." Jay laughed as he kept walking.

Nivea was still standing by the fridge, afraid to move; now that Von had come in, she was even weaker in the knees. She began to eat on the ice chips as if they were her last meal, trying to look around the immaculate kitchen as if he wasn't there.

Von made him a plate of spaghetti and grabbed a couple of pieces of chicken. Nivea watched as Von put his plate in the microwave. He then took a swig of his beer. When the microwave stopped, Von grabbed his plate and a fork. Nivea let out a relieved breath when Von began to leave out of the kitchen. In mid-stride he stopped, turned around, and walked over toward Nivea.

Her heart was beating a mile a minute. It clearly felt as if it was about to jump out of her chest. Von could see the uneasiness on her face, and used it to his advantage. He walked up and stood directly in front of her. He leaned his body against the breakfast nook and looked her over. *She isn't looking too good,* he thought. He assumed she was uneasy about him and his brother being there.

"What's up?" Von sat his beer on the counter and began to eat from his plate. "So you meant what you said on my answering machine?"

Nivea tried looking over him to see if anyone was walking in, but she couldn't see.

"Yes, I meant it," she said through tight teeth.

"So you're telling me that you're cool on the dick?"

"What? Are you serious? I will not have this conversation with you. How dare you!" She couldn't believe Von.

Von took a forkful of the spaghetti. "How dare I what?" he asked, chewing the remainder of the food.

"Have some respect."

"You weren't talking that respect shit when you were fucking me in my brother's bed."

Nivea placed her hand over her chest and her mouth flew open.

"Now, are you sure you no longer want this dick? I can give it to your cousin. She's been checking a nigga out."

"You're such an ass. Get the hell out, now. Get out!" Nivea's voice was louder than she had intended.

Von didn't say a word. He gave her a once-over, then picked up his beer and walked out. Allie was standing in the kitchen entrance, mean-mugging him. He smirked and kept it pushing.

"Nivea Denise, what in the hell is going on between the two of you? And I want the truth!" Allie demanded.

CR80

Von was sitting in the living room, drinking his beer, and staring in a daze. Thinking about Nivea's attitude, and how he wasn't feeling her pushing him away, had him warm inside. *Nigga, you're salty*, Von thought then chuckled. He took a swig from the beer bottle and shook his head at himself. Here he was, a handsome, chocolate dude, with stacks and stacks of paper; a dude who could have any female he wanted and a baby-momma who loved him to death; but he was tripping off his brother's wife. Damn! I'm cold. He shrugged his shoulders.

"I'm about to bounce." He got up from his seat, looked across the room for his brother, and noticed Travis on the phone with a scowl on his face. He and Travis made eye contact, and Von threw his head up. "What's up?" he mouthed. Travis and Von began to walk toward each other.

"Coco said that she just got jumped; she's stranded at the gas station." Travis pulled the phone away from his ear and handed it to Von.

"Where are you and where's my son?" Von questioned.

Hearing Von's voice and his lack of concern for her well-being, caused the tears that Coco had been holding back to fall. She was pissed beyond measure. She'd heard Travis tell him that she'd been jumped, and the nigga couldn't even ask her if she was o.k.?

"My son is fine. Put Travis back on the phone." She didn't even want to talk to him. Hearing his voice made her sick.

"I said, where are you?"

"Tell Travis to hurry up and, nigga, fuck you!" She ended the call.

"She is ignorant. Let's go," Von said, and handed Travis the phone. "Nothing better have happened to my son," he added as he walked toward the door.

This nigga, thought Travis as he followed behind his cousin. Once they were outside, Travis advised Von that he was taking his own ride. He told him the gas station where Coco was, and they bounced.

It took about twenty minutes to get the gas station. When they got there, the police were talking to Coco, and a tow truck was parked behind her car. Von slid his gun from his backside and slid it in the glove box. He looked in his rearview mirror, and Travis was posted against his seven-four-five, talking on the phone. Von took note of the way he was staring at Coco the entire time.

For Coco to have been jumped, she wasn't all fucked up. Besides her hair being all over her head, a busted lip, and a few scratches on her face, she was straight. Coco was born and raised in Watts. She had got down with some of the baddest, and she could hold her on.

"What happened?" Von asked as he reached for Little Von, who was asleep in Coco's arms. Coco didn't say a word; she simply rolled her eyes and continued to answer the female officer's questions.

"Who are you?" the male officer asked.

"You tell 'em." Von looked at Coco, then walked toward her car.

"What's wrong with the car?" Von asked the tow truck driver.

"Nothing. I just fixed the flat. Now I'm waiting on one of my boys to come so he can make a spare key to the car."

Von looked back at Coco, who was still talking to the police. "What happened? She got jacked?" he asked.

"From what I gather, she got jumped by some girls. Her keys and purse was stolen by a crackhead who was helping her change her flat." The tow driver looked up and noticed his boy's truck pulling into the gas station. "That's the locksmith, right there," said the tow driver.

Von walked over to Travis, who was just hanging up his phone. He told him what had happened, and they waited until the police wrapped it up with Coco so they could get more details.

"We doubt that your purse will show up. If it does, I'm sure that your things won't be in there; but we'll keep an eye out," the female officer informed her. She added, "But I will make it my business to look for the creep who took your things. He won't be too far from here." The guy who Coco and the witnesses had describe was a well-known panhandler in the area.

"What about the tape? Are you guys going to look at that?" asked Coco.

"The attendant doesn't have a key to the box. Her boss will call us later so we can look at it. The only thing is that it's a rolling camera, meaning that the camera does not record the entire station at once. It may record on that corner," the officer pointed west "for five minutes, then at that corner," the officer pointed north, "for three minutes. But don't worry, we know who he is."

"O.k.," Coco replied.

The officer handed Coco her card. "We'll call you, and you can call us if you need us."

"Thanks." Coco began to walk toward her car. The locksmith had finished making her spare key, and her tire had been changed. Coco was handed her key and told that Von had already paid the invoice.

"Thanks, you two," Coco said to the locksmith and the tow driver. She then reached for her baby.

"I've got him. Travis, get the car seat. I'll follow you to the house," said Von.

"For what? I can take my son home. I don't need you to come over."

"I don't give a fuck. I wanna know what the fuck you got yourself into that put my son's life in danger."

Coco took a deep breath. She was already pissed about the two incidents that had taken place, and now this nigga was talking shit. She took another calming breath, and looked at Von.

Travis saw the fire in her eyes and immediately spoke up to defuse the situation. "Coco, just go to the house. We're on the way." Travis placed his hand on the small of her back.

She nodded her head and hopped in the car. As soon as she shut the door, she broke down and cried. She couldn't believe Dre was the cause of her getting jumped, and that Von didn't even care enough to ask her if she was she alright.

"Don't cry," Travis whispered, slid the car seat from the backseat, and shut her door.

"Nigga, that's your baby-momma." Travis shook his head at Von. "At least you could have asked her if she was alright." Travis walked over to Von's ride and secured Little Von's car seat in the back.

"Man, I ain't thinking about Coco. She is always into some shit. Did you forget she's fucking the enemy?"

"But you are thinking about Nivea though?" Travis didn't even bother to look at Von to see his reaction. "Nigga, I ain't stupid," he added, and walked to his car.

Von couldn't do anything but chuckle. That nigga Travis paid attention to everything. He wasn't tripping off Travis telling his brother. He knew he wouldn't.

When they got to Coco's house, she finally told them everything that had happened, leaving out the part about Dre's niece claiming Little Von looked like Dre. With each detail, Von got even more heated.

"You fucking with them squares could have gotten your ass killed and my baby hurt!" He walked up on her and Travis jumped between them.

"Come on. That nigga probably was mad because you made him look like a bitch at the club. She's been through enough. She doesn't need to be hearing you blame shit on her. Let's go handle that nigga." Travis stared into Von's eyes.

Von looked at Coco, who was standing there with her arms folded. "I ain't gotta worry about you fucking with him no more because, on my son, that nigga is dead. But I tell you this: If you ever put my son's life in danger again, I will take yours."

"GET THE FUCK OUT, NIGGA! THE LIFE THAT YOU LIVE PUT YOUR ENTIRE FAMILY IN DANGER. DID YOU FORGET IT WAS YOU THEY WANTED? THAT'S WHY YOUR BROTHER ALMOST DIED!"

Travis had no time to catch his fall. Von had pushed him out of the way and grabbed Coco by the neck by the time Travis got up from the floor. Coco's legs were dangling in the air, and her face looked as if she was about to take her last breath. Travis rushed over and grabbed Von.

"Let's go, man. That's your baby-momma. Your son is right here."

Von still had her in the air. "If you ever in your life come at me like that again, Coco, I will kill you. You're a stupid ghetto bitch."

He released his grip, letting Coco to fall to the floor. Coco sat on the floor, coughing and gagging. Travis pulled Von by the arm out of the door.

Chapter Fourteen

Coco

It took an hour for Coco to pull herself together. As she got up from the hardwood floor, she vowed that she was going to get revenge on all of their asses—the bitches who had jumped her, Dre, and Von.

First on her list was Dre. She hoped that the females would be at his spot. That way she could kill two birds with one stone. After calling her homegirls from the neighborhood where she grew up and a few of her down-ass cousins, she contacted her next door neighbor to watch the baby.

Dressed in jeans, Timberlands, and a black hoodie, Coco stood in front of the house waiting on her "ride-or-dies"; her crew pulled up two cars deep. Coco walked over to the first car, a black Nissan Armada. "Thanks for coming, y'all," she told the five girls. She gave each one of them dap.

"Bitch, it ain't a problem. We got you," said the driver, who they called Shaky.

"You wanna hit this?" The passenger, Brazy, passed Coco the blunt; she took a few hits, then passed it back to them.

She looked in the back at Mia. "Let me get a shot of that." Mia passed her the Remy bottle, and Coco took it to the head. "Alright, follow us." She raised the Remy bottle. "I'm taking the rest of this."

"I got another one for later; don't trip," said Mia.

"Cool." Coco walked over and got in the car with her two cousins, NaeNae and Apple. No words were exchanged. They all knew what time it was. Shit was about to get real. Apple, the driver, turned up the radio, and Little Wayne blasted through the speakers. Already knowing the destination, she driver pulled off with the Armada following behind.

CR80

Von and Travis

"It's like this. We're going up in that bitch, and killing any and everybody." Von looked over at Travis, who was staring into the darkness. Travis' mind was all over the place. He had a lot going on, and had yet to figure out how long it would take to put everything in place.

"Nigga, you sleep?" Von asked.

Travis looked over at Von. "Do it look like it?" He shifted in his seat. "I'm trying to figure out how we're going to go in this

222

nigga's hood, knock on his door, and kill everybody. As soon as they see us coming, niggas are going into survival mode."

Von didn't say anything. Travis was right and he knew it. He was just mad that that nigga Dre had crossed the line—again!"

"So I guess we're going to just sit right here? The niggas are taking too long, and they ain't answering the phone." Von and Travis were parked down the street from Dre's spot. They were waiting on the other goons to roll up. It had already been an hour and the niggas hadn't showed.

"Something probably happened. I hope it didn't." Travis thought about his homies getting caught up by the police or something.

"Me, too, but I can't wait any longer." Von started the truck. They still hadn't confirmed their plan, but Travis said, "Fuck it," and allowed Von to do him. Travis cocked his gun back and relaxed in the seat. At a normal speed, Von rolled down the street.

"These niggas having a gathering or something? "Travis said when he noticed a bunch of people in the street.

"Awww, it's some beef shit. It looks like they're fighting or about to fight." Von looked over at Travis and gave him a head nod. "Nigga, we're about to walk up, and let this nigga have it; they ain't paying attention to us."

"It's your call." Travis let out an aggravated breath. He was ready to get the shit over with.

 CRSO

Coco and Her Crew

When Coco and her girls jumped out the car, there were a few of Dre's homeboys standing on the porch. One of the YG's noticed that Coco was with the girls. Instead of him giving his big homie a heads up, he crossed his arms and waited for the shit to unfold.

"What's with these bitches?" one of the other dudes questioned. He added, "They look like they're ready to fuck somebody up. Whose hoes are they?"

"That's Dre's bitch," the dude said. "The homegirls jumped her today. I don't know what the fuck she thought, coming to the hood like she's about to set some shit off." He nudged his head to the van across the street from them. "The homegirls are posted in the Astro."

He noticed the thick cloud of smoke coming from the van. He hoped his homegirls weren't already fucked up. That PCP was a cold drug. It can have some of the toughest niggas on stuck if they've had too much of it; then there was no doubt that Coco and her girls were going to serve them.

"Where is Dre? Tell him Coco is out here," she said, standing in front of the gate.

"Dre's busy but the homegirls are right there." Dude unfolded his arms and pointed across the street to the van. Coco and her homegirls turned and looked in the direction he was pointing.

"Watch out," one of the young dudes said. As he and his two homeboys mobbed out of the gate, Coco and her girls followed dudes as they ran across the street.

"Y'all get back. Ain't no jumping on my homegirls. Get back over there. Let them get out."

One of the dudes pushed Apple, and hell broke loose. Coco and Brazy rushed the dude who had pushed Apple, while the others jumped on the dudes who were trying to help their homeboy.

Seeing that her homegirls were handling there's for the moment, Apple began to kick on the van. "Why y'all bitches ain't getting out?" Bamm! Bamm! She kicked the van again. "Get out all y'all bitches jumped my homegirl."

The girls were stuck on stupid, the PCP having taken over their minds. They were unfazed in another world as Apple banged on the van.

Dre heard the commotion and ran to the door. "What the fuck is y'all doing?" He pulled his gun from his waist. He and one of his homeboys ran across the street.

"Get the fuck back." Man-Man snatched Brazy off his homeboy. She turned and swung on him. Brazy was a big girl, but she was no match for a real man. Man-Man knocked her out with one punch. By this time, Dre had Coco with her arms pinned behind her back.

"Get your bitch-ass off me, nigga. Let me the fuck go." She tried to break loose but couldn't.

"Shut the fuck up. I ain't letting shit go." He looked at Man-Man. "Stop that shit," Dre said, talking about the girls who were fighting his other two homeboys.

Man-Man pulled his gun from his waist and aimed it in the air. Boc . . . Boc . . . He let two off in the night.

Von and Travis saw Man-Man aim in the air. Right after he put his gun down, the two began to shoot their guns. Dre looked to his right and saw Von and Travis walking his way, shooting. He grabbed Coco and used her as a shield. Boc . . . Boc . . . He shot back. As he was backing up, trying to get away, he tripped over Man-Man's lifeless body and fell backwards. Everyone was screaming and ducking for cover. Coco took off running toward the car.

"Go get Coco," Travis yelled to Von. "I'm 'bout to dead this nigga. Get Coco, nigga," Travis yelled as he ran Dre's way.

It seemed like every one had disappeared, and it was just he and Travis out there. Travis walked up on Dre and began shooting the remainder of his bullets at him.

Dre closed his eyes and began to repent. He knew he had to go, and more than likely it would be by the hands of another man, he just hadn't thought it would be Travis.

"Let's go, nigga." Von swooped up on Travis.

As Travis was running to get in the truck, he saw a nigga peep his head from the side of the van. Boc.. . boc . . . boc . . . He shot the van up and Von punched out. Sirens were heard miles away.

Von hit a quick left on Eighth Avenue, causing the truck to jerk from side to side, and Von almost losing control. He immediately got control of the vehicle, and stepped on the gas. Doing ninety miles per hour, Von was out of the neighborhood within five minutes.

"Let me out of this car. Take me back to my homegirls," Coco yelled.

Von ignored her. His focus was on getting out of the area quickly and safely. His concern wasn't the niggas who he had just shot at; his fear was the police.

"Coco, sit your ass back and chill," Travis demanded.

Coco turned and looked at Travis, "No, fuck that. Y'all should have left me out there. My homegirls are back there." She turned and looked at Von. "Pull this bitch over."

"Bitch, shut the fuck up." Von backhanded Coco and her head flew against the window.

Coco launched at him and began swinging. With one hand, Von tried getting Coco off him, and with the other, he was steering the truck. As Travis pulled Coco off Von, Von's truck ran up on a curb, and knocked over newspaper stand.

"You stupid." He put the car in park. "Get the fuck out, now." Von reached over and slapped Coco in the face. Her lip instantly swelled up.

"Let's go, man," Travis said, looking behind to make sure the police weren't coming. "Coco, shut the fuck up and sit back," Travis ordered. "Von, get the fuck up out of here."

Von put the truck in reverse and backed up all the way down the street. The first block he got to, he hit a sharp left; two blocks down, he jumped on the freeway.

"What the fuck were you doing over there? How you feel about your nigga getting smoked tonight." Von taunted.

Coco stayed quiet. *Pop!* Coco's head jerked to the side. Von hit her again. "Keep your hands off me," Coco cried.

"Naw, fuck that. You were just talking big shit. Oh, you crying because your nigga dead. Thank Travis," Von laughed.

Coc crossed her arms and shook her head. Although she was mad at Dre, she didn't want him dead, and especially not on her watch. The car fell silent; everyone was lost in his or her own thoughts.

Travis was thinking about the consequences of his actions. Von was thinking how he was happy that that nigga Dre was out the picture. Not only did he think Dre was a bitch-ass nigga, but he was low-key jealous when he'd found out that Coco was messing with him. Coco was scared and worried. She didn't know if her homegirls and cousins were safe. On top of that, she knew she had to move. If Dre homeboys knew that Von had something to do with their boy's death—and she believed they did—they were going to come after her.

Von pulled up in front of Coco's house. "Go get my son." He got out the car and waited for Coco.

"You go. I ain't going over there looking like this," she said, referring to her busted lip.

Von took a deep breath. "Go pack some shit up. You ain't staying here tonight. Travis, go with her," Von ordered, then turned and walked off toward the neighbor's house.

Maybe he does care, thought CoCo, *but fuck him. It's too late for all that.* Although Coco was feeling hate toward Von and wanted nothing to do with him, she feared for her safety, so she didn't go against his demands.

"Are you alright? Travis asked when they'd made it into the house.

"I'm fine." She turned to Travis. "Thanks for everything."

Travis threw his hand up as if he didn't know what she was talking about.

"Thanks for answering your phone when I called. Thanks for saving my life." Tears began to fall from her eyes. "I heard you scream, 'Get Coco.' I truly believe that, if you hadn't, Von would have left me out there."

"That's not true," Travis assured her.

"Yeah, whatever." Coco walked over and picked up her house phone. She needed to make sure her folks were alright.

Travis watched her as she talked on the phone. He had much respect and mad love for Coco. She was cool to be around when they all kicked it; she stayed with the jokes. She had also proved her loyalty to Von on several occasions. No matter how many times the nigga cheated or neglected her, she made it her duty to stay by his side. Instead of giving up on them, she fought harder to prove her love. Yeah, she got out of hand a lot of times, but she was a woman scorned. She deserved that right.

Travis walked out of the living room into the kitchen. When he came back, Coco was just hanging up the phone. Travis handed her a napkin filled with ice.

"Thanks." She took the napkin and placed it on her lip. "Ouch," she mumbled.

"What happened? Are they straight?" Travis asked.

"Yeah, they're good." Coco got ready to tell him what had happened, but her phone rang. As she answered the phone, Von walked in with the baby on his arm. Hearing the news, her eyes got big and her heart dropped. She didn't know whether she should tell Von or keep it to herself.

"Who's that?" he asked.

"Apple."

Von didn't think anything of it. "Get off the phone so you can pack."

"Apple, I'll call you later. Thanks, girl. I love you. Bye." She hung up the phone. Her burden had just gotten heavier.

Riding in the car with Von and Travis, Coco wondered where the hell he was taking her. JayVon and Travis were the only family he had, and she knew damn well he wasn't taking her to his house, maybe to Travis' house. When they pulled into some townhouses located in the city of Carson, Coco decided to ask, "Who stays here?"

Von didn't say a word. He simply hit the garage opener and pulled his truck into it.

Travis got out and opened the back door for Coco. He grabbed one of the bags from the trunk and Von grabbed the other. When Coco stepped out the truck, she looked over at the car parked on the other side of the garage and shook her head. She didn't want to ask because she knew the answer would piss her off. Coco picked Little Von up out of the car seat and went into the house.

As soon as she walked in, she saw a picture of Von, JayVon, and Travis on the wall, and became warm. "Who stays here?" She followed them up the stairs.

Von dropped her bag on the floor and looked at Coco. "This is my shit. Ask me no questions and I tell you no lies." He walked into the kitchen, leaving Coco to stand there looking dumbfounded. Von grabbed him and Travis a beer, and walked back into the living room. "Here." He handed Travis his beer.

"Coco, don't go through none of my shit. I'll be back in a few hours." Without looking at her, he walked off. Travis gave her a warm smile, then followed behind his cousin. When Coco heard the garage open, she looked around the house and burst into tears. She couldn't believe the nigga had a whole other life.

Chapter Fifteen

Nivea and Jay

Nivea jumped up out of the bed and ran straight to the bathroom, almost tripping over a pair of shoes she had kicked off the previous night before hopping into bed. She flipped the switch, turning on the light, and hovered over the toilet. It seemed that everything she'd eaten from the past week was coming out of her, as if she hadn't let everything out the previous night. She was too sick to show any affection to Jay.

Trying to ignore the pain, Jay slowly got out of the bed to check on his wife. When he made it to the bathroom, Nivea was on her hands and knees, with her face in the toilet.

"Beauty, are you okay? Jay sat on the side of the tub, rubbing her back.

"Yes, I think it might be something I ate yesterday. She held onto the side of the sink and began to pull herself up. Jay stood up and placed his good arm under her arm to try to help her up.

"Baby, no, I know you want to help, but you're too weak right now. Your body is not fully healed. You can't be doing anything extra."

He frowned at the word weak. "Niv, I'm good," he assured her. He understood where she was coming from, but he still didn't like the word. No matter how much pain he was feeling, it was his duty to take care of his wife. He was going to do just that.

Quickly pulling herself together, Nivea walked out of the bathroom and back into their room.

"Niv, I'm just trying to help," he said, following her back into the bedroom.

Nivea didn't realize she had sounded a bit harsh: she had an attitude and she couldn't understand why. Feeling bad, she turned around, wrapped her arms around his neck, and gave him a peck on the lips.

"Baby, I know you want to help; I just need to be there for you right now. I don't want you to make things worse. It will be a while before your body is completely healed."

She had missed him, and was glad he was home. She thought it would be easy to fall back on track, but if what she believed was the reason for her constant vomiting, she knew that things were bound to change.

Nivea wrapped her arms around Jay's neck and looked into his eyes, "Baby, I love you more than life. I'm so happy to feel your skin brush against mine." She kissed him. "And the feeling of you kissing me back. I even missed seeing your forehead wrinkle when you're slightly mad, but won't say anything. I missed picking up your T-shirts when you throw them next to the laundry basket instead of in it," She smiled. Jay laughed; he was sure she'd seen the white one that was there now, the one he had taken off the previous night. "I needed you so much, baby." A few tears dropped. "I'm sorry, I don't mean to cry. I just . . I don't know," she said, squeezing him tightly.

Nivea didn't know what to say. She knew what needed to be said, but those words would never come out of her mouth. She wanted badly to apologize for sleeping with his brother. She felt awful knowing that he would never cheat on her. But there's she was—every chance she had—eagle spread, allowing Von to fill her up.

Even after the phone call from the hospital informing them that Von was awake, they had continued to betray Jay. They had gone to visit him and, for sure, she'd thought that would be the last of their sex escapades; but, later that night, as Jay slept, she'd slid out of the hospital and met up with Von at the closest hotel. Then every other night after that was a repeat.

"I'm here now, Beauty. I will never leave you again." Jay assured her. "Hey, stop all that crying. You how I feel about you crying. He took her hand, led her to the bed, and she lay down. Jay got in bed with her. He pulled her into his arms and held her until she fell asleep.

CRSO

I have to get some fresh air, he thought. Not feeling like being closed in any longer, and with Nivea sick and sleeping, he had the perfect excuse to leave the house. *Maybe I'll call the hospital and see how Nurse Brandy is doing.* His last few weeks in the hospital, Jay had looked forward to seeing Brandy and talking with her. Jay got dressed, grabbed the keys to the Jag, and decided to go for a much-needed ride before he hit up the grocery store to pick up Nivea some soup and crackers.

CRSO

Brandy

"Here you go, Mommy's stanka. This is the last one," Brandy said, handing Junior the last Flintstone Gummy vitamin. "Since Mommy is off today, you can help me with the laundry; then we can go for a walk." She bent down close to him. "I don't feel like being in the house with Daddy," she whispered. "Don't you want to go for a walk too?

"Yeaaaa, walk, Mommy!" Junior jumped up and down.

"Okay, as soon as we finish the laundry, we're going to leave."

"Lawndry, Mommy, we gon do lawndry first?" he asked, trying his best to pronounce laundry.

"Yes, stanka, laundry first." She kissed him on his cheeks before he took off running into the bedroom, excited about doing laundry with his mother. "Hmmm." She shook her head. "I'll bet he's not this excited when he grows up."

She went into the laundry room and set the water temp, the load size, and dropped two cups of Gain washing powder in the water. She took the stepping stool and set it against the washer so that Junior could load it. That was his job when he helped, and he loved it.

"Okay, Junior, it's ready," she yelled down the hall, waiting to see him come running down the hall, like he'd won an award, with a big smile plastered on his face.

"The watda lukewarm, now?"

"Yes, the water is on and lukewarm. All you have to do is drop the clothes in. Oh, hold on. Mommy needs to get the clothes Daddy had on last night. I'll be right back."

She walked into the bedroom and grabbed his clothes off the floor on the side of the bed. Rob was still sleeping, and she was glad of that. *I have peace and quiet when he's asleep,* she thought, looking at him stretched out on the bed like he didn't have a care in the world.

You deserve better, Brandy. He treats you that way, not because he loves you, but because he loves being in control of you. As long as you allow him to beat you, he will. Get out while you're still alive. Jay words constantly played back in her head.

That's why she'd been kind of resisting him lately. Brandy thought about waking him and confronting him about taking her car the previous night while she and Junior were asleep. He knew damn well he didn't have any money to put gas in the tank. "Lazy bastard," she mumbled.

Brandy got ready to walk out the room when the flashing light from his cell went off. Never one to search through his phone, but curious as to why the ringer was off, she picked it up and took it back to the laundry room with her.

"You have Daddy's clothes, Mommy?"

"Yes, and you did such a good job, too. Now how about you go into your room and let me finish up here. It's time for Blue's

Clues to come on." Junior hopped down, happy to go back to his room to see Blue, his favorite cartoon character.

"Walk, Junior, before you fall and hurt yourself."

"Otay," he said, still running.

Junior was very smart and she didn't want him to mention around his father that she had his phone.

"What am I looking for? There's no way he would ever cheat He is too crazy about me," she told herself, feeling bad about what she was about to do. "Hell, I pay the bill. I have every right!"

She set the phone down on the dryer and emptied his pockets before putting his clothes into the washer. She pulled a piece of gold paper from his pocket. "What the hell is this?" She examined the paper as best she could; it could have been anything. Thinking that it might be a piece of a condom wrapper, her heart began to beat faster.

She pulled his pants back out of the washer, trying to make sure that she hadn't missed anything else in his pockets. His pockets were empty, so she put them back in water. Brandy sat on the side of the washer, and began to scroll through Rob's call log. His cousin John's name popped up five times today and four times yesterday, around the same time she and Junior had gone to sleep.

'Why does John keep calling so much? Rob, what the hell do you have going on? You'd better not be selling drugs again."

She opened a text message:

I wish you were still here. This kitty cat is still purring. You really made her talk back last night :) 8:00 am from John

See she can't love you like I do. I had you first and when we were together you never had any curfew. Fuck her come home. 8:15 am from John

Baby I need a ride to work at 5 pm. Can you come pick me up? If so get here at @3 so you can taste the kitty. I'm horny and soaking wet think about you. 8:30 am from John

Brandy felt sick to her stomach, but it was nothing compared to the fire running through her body. All the falsely accusing her of cheating and he was the one cheating! She was pissed. How could he be so ungrateful after all she done? So selfish, so disrespectful, and to have the bitch up in her car? Brandy lost it. She stormed to the bedroom, pushed the door open, causing it to slam against the wall. Rob jumped up from his sleep.

"What's going on?" he asked. Before he knew it, Brandy had dived on top of him, raining blow after blow.

"I hate you! I hate you! I hate you! You selfish muthafucka."
She was screaming, yelling, and swinging on him like a wild
animal. "Why do you beat me? Why don't you just stay with that
bitch if you love her so much? I trusted you. I trusted everything
you said." She clawed at his face. Rob tried to grab her arms, but
she was going in on him. He'd never seen her that way.

"Get the hell off of me."

Rob pushed Brandy with enough force to cause her to fall to
the floor. The shove didn't faze Brandy. Rob had beaten her so
much, she was use to it, and the anger and hurt she was feeling had
her numb. Brandy jumped up from the floor, ran over to the other
side of the bed, and grabbed the lamp, causing a picture of her and
Rob to fall off the dresser.

Rob raised his hands to cover his face. "You better not hit me
with that lamp."

Brandy hurled the lamp at him, hitting him in the chest. Then
she ran and jumped back on top of him. He pushed her off him
again and she fell to the floor.

"You sick, retarded bastard, I hate you." Brandy ran over to
the chest of drawers, and grabbed perfume and cologne bottles.
She began tossing them at Rob. Brandy was crying profusely. Snot

and tears were all over her face. All the years of abuse and this is the thanks she got. She was devastated.

He'd hurt her to the core, and he knew it. Instead of trying to fight her, he tried talking to her. "Baby, wait. What are you talking about? I'm not cheating. "

"Oh yeah? Then what the fuck is this?" She grabbed the cell from the floor and threw it at him. "Fuck you, Rob, I want you out. Now!"

Rob ran up on her and grabbed her by the arms. Brandy was fighting and kicking so hard that Rob had to wrestle her to the floor.

"Get off me. I don't ever want your filthy hands touching me again."

"Calm the fuck down Brandy. Look, I don't give damn what's in that phone. It's probably just some bitch playing games. Did you see any outgoing messages? Hell, naw! You know why? Because I don't fuck with no other bitch. I know you're hurt so I'mma leave so you can calm down and think about how you overreacted. I'll be back." He kissed her cheek, let her go, and walked out of the room, leaving her balled up on her side, crying her heart out.

"Lord, why? What could I have done so wrong to deserve this treatment? Why, when I give my all, am I treated as a doormat?" Brandy lay there for thirty minutes, crying her heart out and questioning God, but she didn't listen for an answer. Once she'd gathered enough strength to get up, she went to check on her son. There was a note on the bed. *I took Jr with me. I'll call you later and I love you. ~ Rob*

"I bet you do," she said ripping up the note and tossing the torn pieces of paper in the air. "He thinks taking my baby with him is going to help him? Oh, hell no, it's not! I'm going to get my baby and leave his cheating ass right at his mammy's house." She marched into her room yanked open all of Rob's dresser drawers, and emptied all of his belongings onto the bed.

"You want to cheat on me after all I have done? Fuck waiting for you to treat me right. I deserve better." She went into the kitchen, grabbed five large garbage bags, and went back into their bedroom to bag up everything that belonged to him, while cursing and yelling as if he were still there. "You want to have some off-brand, butch-looking bitch riding in my shit? You want the hoe, then you can have her, and leave me and my child the hell alone.

She packed up the last of his clothes and threw them in the backseat of her car. Not giving a damn that she still had a scarf tied around her head, and had on a halter top and short shorts, she threw on her white Nikes, grab her keys, and headed over to his mother's house.

Chapter Sixteen

Nivea and Jay

An hour later, Nivea woke up feeling for Jay on his side of the bed; he wasn't there. "Baby, where are you?" Nivea got up from the bed and went to the bathroom. After emptying her bladder, she washed her hands, then her face, and brushed her teeth. *Lord, when will this sickness end,* she thought as she made her way downstairs in search of her husband.

"Baby, where are you?" she called out. When she didn't get an answer, she looked over at the key rack and noticed that the keys to the Jag were gone. She thought, *Where could he have gone?* She picked up the house phone and called him.

Jay had just pulled into the grocery store lot and killed the engine when his cell rang.

"S'up, Beauty? You're awake?"

"Where are you? You should not be out of bed already. It's only the second day you've been out the hospital. You'd better not be anywhere near Good Deeds Real Estate," she lectured her hardheaded husband. Getting a little nervous, but more upset, Nivea began to pace back and forth.

Jay smiled knowing she was pissed and probably walking in circles. "Now, Beauty, calm your nerves. I'm on my way in the store. I just dropped off my prescription at the pharmacy. I'm alright."

"JayVon, I could have dropped your prescription off for you. You didn't have to leave. How long have you been gone?" she asked, looking at the clock on the microwave, wondering how long she'd been asleep.

"About thirty minutes; I needed some air. I'll be back in a few minutes. How are you feeling? Do you need anything from the store?"

"I feel better, and we don't need anything. I went shopping before you came home."

"I know you're on top of things. I just didn't want you to have to get up and cook breakfast for me, so I thought about stopping by IHop on my way to the store to get you crackers and soup. Just in case you have a taste for them later, I'll bring you back some bagels with strawberry cream cheese."

Jay knew just how to keep her mouth shut. Nivea loved cream cheese and bagels, and often sent him on a late night trip to her favorite place to get them. "Well, mister, in that case, you'd better hurry back with my cinnamon bagels. You have less than twenty minutes to get here."

"Ha ha . . . Okay, I love you."

"I love you more and hurry home."

Nivea placed the phone on the counter and headed back upstairs. She heard the ringing of her cell phone, but knew it wasn't her husband so she didn't rush to get it. Once she made it into the room, she picked it up off the nightstand and saw that she had a few missed calls. The first one was from Allie; the other two were from Von. She blew out a deep breath from her mouth and placed one hand on her forehead. She was pissed off.

"Why in the hell does he keep calling? He knows damn well this can't be happening. Ughhhh!" she yelled out in frustration and lay back on the bed. She wanted to call Von, but she was scared and still upset with him because of the way he acted at Jay's welcome-home party. He'd made her so nervous and uncomfortable that she knew her husband had to have noticed how uneasy she felt. Nivea hated that her husband was gone, but she needed a few minutes to herself to think things over.

She walked into the bathroom and turned the water on to fill up the tub. Once it was half-full, she removed her robe. *This should help me to relax. I'll take a hot bath first, then call Allie back after. Why didn't I just wait until my husband came out of his coma? Why did I take it there with Von?* she thought as she eased her body into the warm water.

CRISO

Jay went to Albertsons grocery store and bought Nivea crackers, soup, bagels, and cream cheese. He really wasn't in the mood for stopping by IHop. He'd only said that to buy him more time to ride around.

How in the hell did I get mixed up in this street life shit? I know it wasn't an accident. I bet them niggas were looking for Von. He just doesn't want to tell me. Jay tried hard to remember the faces, but he couldn't remember much besides hearing a lot of shots. He knew Von was on a manhunt, but a part of him want to tell him to pull back. He didn't want anything to happen to his brother. As his mind continued to wander, he saw a car on the side of the road with the emergency lights flashing; the woman slamming the door was obviously pissed. *Wait, is that who I think it is?* he thought as he made a quick U-turn.

CRISO

Brandy

After she'd gotten a couple miles down the street, she'd looked at the gas gauge, and it instantly raised her temper a couple of notches. "DAMN IT! DAMN IT, DAMN YOU!" Brandy yelled, pushing on the gas pedal and hitting the steering wheel, hoping that the car would keep going. As many times as she pumped the pedal, it only got her another block before she had to pull over to the side of the road. "Great! Just fucking great!"

She looked over at the passenger seat, ready to grab her purse so that she could take her phone out to call Rob and curse him the hell out. After seeing the seat was empty, she cursed herself for not bringing her purse. She was now boiling hot that she had to get out of her car and walk down the street in a pair of booty shorts and a tank top. She opened the door, got out, and slammed it behind her, accidentally locking the keys in the car. "Shit! This not my fucking day."

She yanked off her scarf and stuffed it in her back pocket. Noticing a Jag doing a U-turn in the street, she looked at her reflection through the window, trying to straighten out her hair. *I hope he'll give me a ride for free. Please don't be someone who knows me.* The Jag pulled in front of her, and out stepped the last person she wanted to see her looking like this. Brandy could have passed out. *Lord, no, why did it have to be Von when I look tore up,*

"Hi, Von," she said, smiling nervously.

"How could you forget me so soon?" he said, smiling.

Damn! I could just melt in that smile. He is so sexy. Focus, Brandy, focus, she coached herself. She cleared her throat. "What do you mean? Forget you? How could I?" She batted her long lashes.

"So why are you calling me Von? You know I heard there was a dude going around town acting and looking like me," he chuckled.

"Ohhhh, Mr. JayVon Deeds." Brandy put her hand on her chest. "I didn't know that you were out of the hospital. Oh my, you look so different. I thought you were your brother."

Jay could have said the same about her. She, too, looked different out of her scrubs. In fact, she wasn't looking half-bad in the gear that he thought should only be worn in her home, but he kept his comment to himself.

"Wait, hold up." She placed one hand up in the air and the other one on her hip. "What are you doing out of the house? You shouldn't be outside so soon." She went into nurse mode quickly.

"I know you haven't been out that long because I've only been gone a week. I'm on vacation," she quickly added to clear up any domestic issues that may have crossed his mind.

"Naw, I'm good! I just went to drop my prescription off and now I'm headed back home." He glanced at her car. "What's up with your ride?"

"Well, um . . ." She held her head down a shame. "I ran out of gas, and I left my purse home. I was so frustrated once I realized that I'd left my purse at home that I got out of the car, locked the door before slamming it, then noticed that I'd left my keys in the car.

"One of those days, huh?"

Brandy let out a long breath. She stood quiet for the next couple of seconds, her throat burning. She felt emotional just thinking about all the things she'd continued to put up with, and how foolish he'd made her look once again.

"I can call AAA, or if you're in a hurry, I can take you where you going."

The sound of Jay's voice broke her out of her thoughts. "Oh no, that's okay. If you would take me home, I have a spare key there."

"Okay, no problem; let's go."

Jay opened the passenger door and Brandy got in. Jay got in and pulled off. The first couple of minutes, the ride was awkward. Neither of them spoke a word. Brandy had felt comfortable talking to him while he was in the hospital. She had felt like they were old friends and she knew him well; but seeing him outside of the hospital, she felt nervous for some reason.

"I don't live too far away from here," she said, breaking the silence.

"Can I ask you a question?"

"Sure!"

"Where are you running off to?"

"What makes you think I'm running off somewhere?"

"From the little that you've told me, plus what I can see, speaks volumes."

"So, me running out of gas and locking my keys in the car says Brandy must be running away?"

"Well, if you add the fact that you rushed off so quickly leaving your purse, something women never do, and the fact that you have a back seat full of bags that I'm sure are filled with clothes. Your mind was so cloudy that you didn't think to check the gas gauge when you got in the car, nor did you take the keys out of the ignition when you stepped out of the car?"

"So what in the hell are you? A psychic or some shit like that?" Now slightly upset that he almost nailed it on the head, Brandy folded her arms across her chest. "I guess you're going to tell my damn future next?" Not giving him a chance to answer, she began to direct him the rest of the way to her house. "Take a left right there, and a right at the next stop light.'

"Whoa, no harm intended! Pump your brakes, ma. I was only asking."

She looked out the passenger-side window, wishing she could take back take the frustration she'd let out on him. It wasn't his fault; he was only asking the obvious.

"Just drop it, o.k.?"

"Done; I never asked you anything."

"Thank you."

"Anyhow, it was funny that I ran into you today. I actually was looking forward to seeing you the day that I left the hospital. I wanted to thank you for all you'd done. If there is ever anything I can help you with, please never hesitate to let me know." He handed her his business card.

"You don't have to thank me, Mr. Deeds. It was my job to take care of you. That's what I went to school for and that's what I'm paid to do."

"Yeah, I understand that, but there's a difference. Some people do it just for the money. I can tell that you do it because you truly care, and when you were helping me, I saw the passion and love you have. People like you, who go the extra mile, should be rewarded. Please don't hesitate to use that card. If you ever start looking for a home, I'd be honored to help."

She took the card out of his hand, and told him to pull up to the building that sat behind hers. She didn't want him to park in front of her building, just in case Rob had come back home.

"Thank you, Mr. Deeds. I'm not always this grouchy," she laughed. "I do have a good heart. It just that I have a lot on my plate right now; I really didn't mean to lash out at you. I'm glad I left a good impression, and you were able to notice the good in me. Don't know if I ever be able to stay out of the hole long enough to be able to afford a home, but if I do, I will use it." She smiled and he gave her a head nod. "Wait right here. I'll be right back. Can I get you something to drink?"

"Naw, I'm good; thank you. There is one thing that I would like for you to do for me."

"And that is?"

"Call me Jay," he said, followed by that perfect smile.

She laughed and stepped out the car then turned back. "How about I call you JayVon?"

"Works for me," he told her.

CRSO

Brandy retrieved her spare key from underneath the flowerpot and hurried into the house to change her clothes. She damn near jumped out of her skin when she saw Rob sitting on the couch.

"Where are going?" Robert's voice boomed. "Naw, fuck that, where are you coming from in those little-ass shorts you got on? Who the fuck are you seeing?"

"Where is Junior? How long you been here?" She ignored his questions.

"Brandy, don't fucking play with me. I'm giving you a chance to answer the damn question before I figure the shit out my damn self. So what it is?"

"If you must know, you used up all the damn gas in the car driving that hoochie around town, never bothering to ask the bitch to the fill up the gas tank. So I ran out of gas and locked the keys in the car. Now I'm here, wondering what the hell are you doing here. I asked you to leave earlier."

"We can talk about that later. How did you get back home, and why did you walk from that way?" He pointed towards the back of the house.

Thinking fast she said. "The bus stop is on the corner and that's how I got home."

"Well, let's catch the bus back up to the car since you supposedly ran out of gas."

"No, Robert, I don't want to be anywhere near you. I'm done. I'm so done with you. Please go home to your bitch. In fact, yeah, you can catch the bus with me because, as soon as I fill up, you can get all your shit out my car and take it to your bitch's house." She began to walk up in his face, pointing her finger, ready to slap the taste out of his mouth again. "I hate that I ever believed you. Why did I ever trust you? You're just a lazy piece of dog shit."

At that last comment, he took her hand, bent it behind her back, and pushed her up against the wall, with her hand balled up in his, squeezing tight. "See, I was trying to be nice about the whole situation, but you're pushing me to hurt you."

"Ahhhh, ouch! Rob, let me go, you're hurting me!"

"Can we sit down and talk like grown-ups, or are you going to insult me and cause me to have to treat you like a baby?"

"O.k., o.k., please just let me go. I'm sorry," she cried. "Just let me go."

He let her loose and turned her so that she would be facing him. He began to wipe the tears from her face. "Baby, I'm sorry. I know I fucked up. I just took the bitch to McDonald's on her dime. Now I do admit that shit, but I didn't fuck her. You've got to believe me that I would never mess up what I have at home."

Brandy's body shook from crying so hard. The pain from Robert bending her hand was nothing compared to the pain in her heart.

"Baby, you know I've been trying. I left earlier so you could calm down. You see I haven't put my hands on you." He wrapped his arms around her, hugging her tight. I took Junior to my brother's house, then came back to check on you. I know you're hurting, and I didn't want to leave you that way. Shhhh, baby, I'm sorry if I hurt you; I swear." Rob searched her eyes for the love that he knew was still there. "I swear on everything I love that I'm not cheating, and you know I ain't going anywhere, so you can give that thought up. We are one, baby. No other man was made for you; nobody's gonna love you like I do." Slowly but surely, Brandy wrapped her arms around him and continued to cry into his chest.

CRSO

Jay

After Jay waited for about thirty minutes, he figured she either wasn't coming back or couldn't. *Maybe that dude is there*, he thought before pulling off. Jay was glad he'd had the chance to thank her, and hoped she would use the business card he'd given her. She'd told him stories about her life growing up, losing her mother at a young age, and the struggle she'd had going to school with no support from her son's father. He didn't like her staying with someone who beat on her. He knew he hadn't known her long, but felt like she was the younger sister he'd never had. He wanted to reach out and help as much as he could.

Driving off, he picked up his phone made a couple of calls to a few roadside assistance friends he had to see who was in the area and could put some gas in her car ASAP. After securing her some gas, he called AAA and purchased her service for three years.

JayVon went back to the car and left a note on it informing her of his good deed.

Jay began to feel the pain and the weakness from staying out and decided to go straight home.

Chapter Seventeen

Nivea and Jay

"Yesss . . . uhhhh . . . Vonnnn . . . Control her. She missed you so much. Ohhhh baby, it's yours; it's all yours. Ahhhh . . . oh, oh . . . yessss . . . Make her talk back to you."

Von thrust in and out of her as he held her tight around the hips. "Are you going to stop fighting me?" he asked, with her one leg propped up on the tub, grunting between words.

"Yes. Yes. Yes. It yours; no more fighting you."

"Act like you mean it; turn around and throw that ass back."

Nivea did as she was told. She assumed the position, bent over, and spread it wide.

"Damn, Nivea! Just like that! Ohhhh . . . shit . . . Nivvvv . . . Damn! That's it."

"Ohhhh baby . . . ohhhh . . . yes, I miss this . . . Von—" Nivea cried out in pure bliss.

"Niv, Niv, Nivea, wake up!" JayVon shook her.

Nivea jumped, almost sliding under in the now-cold bath water. She looked up at her husband as if he were a ghost. Holding her chest, she looked around for any signs of Von. Grateful that it was just a dream, she looked up at her husband and wondered just how much he'd heard.

"Beauty, are you're o.k.? Don't tell me that my brother tormented you to the point that he's bothering you in your dreams, too?" he laughed.

She pouted her lips. "It isn't funny, Jay. He's in my dream talking about my cooking, too. I can't stand his black butt."

"O.k., I'm sorry, baby." He took the towel and wrapped it around her. "I thought you said that the two of you were almost friends now? I'm going to have a talk with about bothering with you."

"No, honey, that's not necessary. I can handle Von any day. To be honest with you, I've learned that he's not that bad of a guy."

"I've heard that before. Your bagels are on the table. I'm going to lay down a minute. O.k., honey?"

As Nivea dried off, she thought about how the dream was so intense that she'd thought it was real. *I have to get him out of my system.* Nivea walked into the room and saw JayVon lying on the bed.

"Honey, are you okay? You don't look well. Are you in pain? Where's your medicine? Let me get it for you."

"Calm down, Beauty, I'm good. I was out too long, that's all. I took a couple of pills that I already had. My prescription won't be ready until later."

"Did you eat anything yet?"

He shook his head no and closed his eyes.

"Jay, you can't take that type of medication without eating first. Let me go fix you something to eat." Nivea left the room to go fix her husband something to eat. She made a mental note to check on Allie and her father.

Chapter Eighteen

Brandy

"Noooo, baby, stopppp. Stop it. Stop it, please. I can't take any more." Brandy had laughed so hard that her stomach hurt and felt like it was about to burst.

"See, Junior, the tickle monster got a hold of Mommy now; tell her to say mercy."

Junior laughed at his mommy squirming around on the picnic blanket while his father tickled her.

"Say it, Mommy, say it. Say mercy, Mommy, say it."

"Okay, mercy, mercy, mercy. You won; now stopppp."

"Yeaaaa, Daddy, Mommy said mercy." He high-fived his dad.

"Junior, that's not right. Why did you let Daddy do that to me?" She pouted as if she was mad.

"Mommy, it's okay to lose sometimes, member? Member you said that? Huh, Mommy?"

They both broke out into laughter, knowing those were her words, exactly. Junior hardly ever forgot anything. His memory was sharp, just like his mother's.

The past few weeks, Robert had tried his best to keep his hands off Brandy. When he was upset, he would go into another room until he felt the anger was gone. He did feel bad about cheating on her. He knew Brandy was good to him; she did everything that he asked and more. *I have to stop messing around on her,* he thought, feeling guilty for lying. Watching her and Junior play kickball, his heart smiled. They were his everything, and he wouldn't know what to do if he ever lost them.

Rob was trying his best to prove that he loved her. He would watch the baby when she went to work, and although he wanted to ask for money, he didn't. He even watched Junior while she hung out with Coco at the club.

Brandy looked over at Rob, and they both smiled. She wondered what he was thinking. *Am I really the one who makes him smile, or is he playing it off and thinking about that ex-bitch of his? It's all good; but I know one thing: I am going to keep a close watch on his ass. He'd better hope I don't see her, because it's on.*

Although she and Rob had a lot to do to repair their relationship, she was grateful that at least he was trying now. Rob had even gone to put in job applications. Brandy knew that it was hard for him not to put his hands on her, especially when she talked mess. She didn't think it was right that he had beaten her the way he had, but she'd made it up in her mind that no relationship was perfect.

"Yo, B, y'all ready to bounce?" Rob looked at his watch.

Brandy and Junior walked over to where he was sitting on the blanket. She got on her knees and kissed him. Rob slid his tongue in her mouth, and they shared a deep, passionate kiss.

"Mmmm," Brandy began to moan.

"Yeah, let's go because, baby, Mommy needs Daddy to put out her fire." She sucked her bottom lip.

"Don't start something you can't finish." Rob wanted to take her right then and there. If Junior wasn't there, he would have. "My mom wants Junior to stay the night; let's go drop him off."

"He's going to be excited. It's perfect timing. We can spend the rest of the day alone." Brandy gave him a wicked smile before getting up. They packed up their blanket and picnic basket, called Junior over, and left.

Their first stop was to drop Junior off, then they headed to the mall. Brandy wanted to get a few things for Junior and Rob out of Burlington.

After they had shopped for a few hours, Brandy decided that she wanted ice cream. Rob didn't know it, but the real reason she wanted to stop was so she could see if Trixie was working today. Brandy had done her homework on his ex, and knew that she worked at the mall at Ice Cream Land. She wanted to see the trick who was sleeping with her man and confront her about it.

Unknown to Brandy, Trixie was having lunch in the food court, not too far from them. She saw her and Rob, and got pissed off.

"B, get me a sugar cone with chocolate ice cream. I have to go take a leak." Rob gave Brandy a peck and walked off.

Brandy hoped that she made it to the front before Rob got back.

CR80

in the hell am I going to get out of this, Rob thought as
pants up. He walked over to the sink and washed his
't even bothered to flush the toilet. When Brandy
he wanted to go to the mall—that mall—he'd

wanted to suggest that they go to a different mall, but that mall didn't have the store Brandy wanted to go in.

He'd thought she would do a little shopping, then be ready to leave. But, no, her ass wanted ice cream. Rob decided to wait around in the restroom a little longer, hoping that Brandy would have ordered and left by the time he got back over there. Just as he took a deep breath, in walked Trixie.

"Girl, what the hell are you doing in here?"

She shut the door and locked it behind her. "Don't start tripping now. I should be the one acting a plum fool. How are you going to bring that fat bitch to my job? What's up with that? And why haven't I heard from you in weeks? Are you playing house with that bitch?" She crossed her arms, waiting on his response.

"Girl, get your ass out of here with that shit. You knew deal; play your part. There's enough meat for everyone grabbed his crouch.

"You are a nasty nigga, but it's cool. You're rig' thing: I will play my part." She turned around and door. "I going to tell the bitch everything out."

"Wait, Trixie, you're trying to mess shit up for the both of us. We can still kick it, but give me some time. Think about it like this: what I get, you benefit from it, too. You know she's about to get me that car, so quit tripping. You need a ride to work, not me." He hugged her from behind and kissed her on her neck.

"I'm not going to wait on you forever, Robert."

Knock knock

"Rob, are you okay? Let's go; that line is too long." Brandy stood there with a gut wrenching feeling that something wasn't right.

"hh. Don't you say anything," he whispered. "Stay in here til I go. I'll call you later. Remember, if you act a fool, fit from what I get."

the bathroom holding his stomach. "Baby, let's oo well."

oney? What do think is going on with your just get ate?"

know how I be that sandwich we ate earlier. Let's y stomach tightens up more. You ic bathrooms anyway."

Rob wanted to act as if he was faking, but the truth was his stomach had actually started to ball up in knots. Not because of the food that he'd eaten earlier, but because Trixie was known to act a fool in the past, and he didn't know how much longer she would stay in the bathroom. Once Trixie's mind was made up about something, it was hard to change it, especially if it had anything to do with something she felt belonged to her.

"O.k., baby, let's hurry and get you home. I hope I don't get sick, too." They turned and headed towards the exit. "Oh, hold on a second." Brandy quickly let go of his hand, spun around in her pumps, and headed towards the bathroom. "I've gotta pee, too."

"Brandy! Brandy, wait!" Rob yelled, walking behind her, hoping she would go into the ladies' restroom, not the family bathroom. "Damnit," he whispered as he watched her snatch open the door and charge her way in.

When Brandy saw her, all she could do was shake her head. She actually felt sorry for the idiot. Here she was, standing there looking crazy, weighing all of one hundred and twenty-five pounds. She wasn't even pretty, especially not with those dark spots all over her face. The makeup she wore didn't even cover it. Her hair was pulled back with an old, drawstring ponytail. She was dressed in an ice-cream-cone apron. He talked about her being fat. Fat or skinny, this bitch had nothing on her.

"Hi, Brandy, it's nice of you to come join me; but, unfortunately, I don't do bitches. Rob should have told you that," Trixie had the nerve to say.

"Nice uniform," Brandy laughed. She turned and looked at Rob. "This is the best you can do? At least give me some competition. Damn! If this is the kind of trailer trash that you want to be with, I'mma let you have that. Neither one of you is worth the fight or my energy. I just needed proof. Y'all bitches can have each other." She turned to walk away.

"If you haven't notice, I never needed nor asked for your permission. Rob has been mine since day one. You played the sideline while I just enjoyed the benefits. Now, who's the dumb bitch?"

"Shut yo stupid ass up, Trixie. None of that shit ever happened. Let's go, B, we can talk in the car."

"Fuck you, Rob. Don't touch me." She yanked her arm away, and with her other hand, slapped the hell outta him. "I'm not going anywhere with you. You can go to hell."

"Baby, this is bullshit. She came in the bathroom when I was using it."

"I don't give a damn what happened. Y'all bitches were made for each other." Brandy shoved Rob in the chest.

"If you put your hands on my man again, you will be leaving out of here in an ambulance."

Brandy thought about all she had to lose. Neither her son nor her nursing license was worth jeopardizing for a nothing-ass girl. She shook the dirt off her shoulders and decided to leave.

"Brandy, wait, it isn't what you think. It's not what it seems like. Please, just let me explain. You know I don't love that hoe."

He followed her in the hallway. Brandy kept going. She felt the tears about to fall, but she refused to let them see her cry. Trixie had had enough; she couldn't stand it any longer watching Rob chase behind her, begging and pleading his case, acting as if she was nothing more to him but a hoe. It made her jealous and outraged.

"Let that hoe go, Robert! You know how she runs and never fights back. She's a scary bitch, anyway." When she saw that she couldn't get a reaction out of Brandy, she added, "That's why Junior loves for me to watch Blue's Clues' movies with him in his room when his mommy is out making our money. He knows the real from the fake and scary."

Brandy turned around and looked at her.

Trixie smiled and rubbed her stomach. "By the way, Rob, I'm late. It looks like Junior will have a brother or sister to—"

She never got a chance to finish her sentence. Brandy charged at her with a two-piece, knocking Trixie on the ground. All that convincing herself not to fight had gone out the door. Trixie was shocked. She thought Brandy couldn't fight and never expected her to hit her like that. She jumped up as if she was Muhammad Ali and threw her set up, jumping around.

Rob decided to sit back and allow Brandy to handle her business. He knew she was about to tear Trixie's ass up, and she deserved it for running her mouth. They went head-to-head, round-for-round, throwing blows, Brandy hitting her target, while Trixie was swinging wild at the air.

Once everyone started to form a crowd around them, the security guard came running. Rob had to pry Brandy off Trixie, and practically drag her out the mall.

"Get your hands off me now. You're a lying son-of-a-bitch, and I hope I stomped that bastard child out of her."

"Baby, that bitch is lying. She ain't pregnant, and if she is, it's not mine. I never fucked her."

"Is there a problem here?" A security guard walked up.

"No, sir, everything is fine. We're just having a little disagreement. We will be leaving right now," Rob said to the short, stubby security guard.

"Yes, there's a problem. I'm trying to get in my car leave, but this sorry, lying-ass nigga don't wanna let me go."

"You have to let her go or I'm calling the cops. Please don't make me do it. Just leave brother."

Ignoring the security guard, Rob looked at her, knowing it was the end for him; but he had meant ever word he'd said to her before. She couldn't leave him. He would never accept it. He would give her some space and a chance to cool off, but she could never leave him. She belonged to him.

"So this is how you're going to do it, Brandy? Just leave me out here like this? How am I going to catch the bus with no damn money?"

Brandy jumped in her car, cranked it up, rolled down her window, and threw out his pack of cigarettes. "Maybe you and your baby-momma can figure that out. You're no longer my problem." She smashed on the gas and pulled out, brokenhearted.

Chapter Nineteen

Later that night at Nivea & Jay's

"Baby, what would you like for dinner?" asked Nivea. She and Jay were sitting in their bedroom. Thinking about the way she'd put it down this morning, he would prefer her rather than her cooking. Not because she was bad at cooking; truth be told, Nivea was getting better with her cooking skills. She'd brought several cookbooks, studied them, and called her father for reassurance. With some guidance from Allie every now and then, she'd been doing pretty well.

"Come here, beautiful," said Jay.

She walked to the side of the bed, and he sat up, tapping the spot next to him, telling her to have a seat. She did.

"Yes, honey?" She saw the serious look on her his face, and the palms of her hands started to sweat. *Oh no, Lord. I hope Von didn't tell! No, he wouldn't do that. Wait, maybe someone saw us. We have been a little careless. Shit, what would I say? Take a deep breath, Nivea, and remember whatever it is, you're innocent until proven guilty.*

"Hear me out, first, before you trip. I've been on lock down too long, and I can't stay another week cooped up in this house, in this room, looking at that TV. I'm just about one second from hating the place that I designed and had built just for us. You know how much I love our home and especially this room, but this," he pointed to the wall, "is driving me nuts. I'm going back to work next week, only two days a week, for now. I will not visit any sites nor will I leave the job to travel to any meetings. I will leave home, go straight to work, handle my business, then back home." He paused so she could digest what he was asking. "Come on, honey, you have to meet me halfway on this. Two days a week," he said, almost begging her to agree. He was hoping she would, to keep the arguing down, because whether she wanted him to or not, he was going back to work.

"Two days a week, huh?"

"Yes, for now, only two."

"You think you're slick, Deeds. Whether I say yes or no, your mind is already made up!"

Jay couldn't hold the laughter in. He pulled her close with his good arm, and planted kisses on her forehead. "That why I love you. You're so understanding."

"Yeah, whatever, smart ass. You'd better not try to go a third day." She got up and asked him again, "What did you want for dinner?"

"Oh, don't worry about that. I ordered pizza since it's my last day of confinement. We're going to party—dinner and a movie. What do you say?"

"Sounds good to me. Can I get you anything?"

"Naw, I'll be down in a second. The food should be here shortly. I called them about forty minutes ago. You may want to change into something a little bit more decent. I would hate to beat up the delivery guy."

"Hmmmm, the delivery guy may have a little more money than you," she teased him, moving her body like a stripper.

"Yo, don't get that kid killed."

Nivea laughed at his jealousy and left to change. She was happy and feeling extremely good today. Von seemed to have finally gotten the memo and stopped calling. She hadn't been sick the last few days. Everything seemed to be falling back in place, like it use to be, even though she knew what lay later on down the road, with the secret she was withholding from both her husband and his brother.

The doorbell rang.

"Get that, honey," Jay called out.

"I heard it; I'm going." She walked to the door, feeling extra nice. The drink she'd made had her mellowed out. If Allie had known she was drinking in her condition, she would have been pissed off.

"Daby, do you have—" She turn the doorknob while yelling over her shoulder, but she stop in mid-sentence as she saw Von standing there, holding three pizzas in one arm and some big-booty chick in the other arm. He even had the nerve to be whispering in her ear. By the look of it, whatever he'd said had her ready to screw him on her porch, by the way she was licking her lips.

Nivea was hotter than fish grease. You would have thought she'd seen her worst enemy by the look on her face. *Who in the hell is this bitch with this fake ass? The nerve of him! He had to be disrespectful and bring the hoe here. Well, he has another think coming; she is not stepping one foot in my house.*

"Can I have the pizzas, please?" she said with much attitude, holding her hand out for the pizzas, and ready to slam the door in their faces.

"Oh, my bad, ma. I didn't notice you had opened the door. This is—"

She cut him off. "You can save the introduction. Just give me the pizzas." Then she felt Jay wrap his arm around her.

"Baby, what's taking so long? Who's at the door?" he played it off. He then looked at his brother. "Ah, man, it's that nigga who's walking around town trying to mirror my good looks."

"You got jokes, kid. You could never look like this." Von rubbed his neatly-trimmed beard.

Now it was Von's date's turn to look crazy in the face. She'd hooked up with Von a time or two, but he'd never mentioned he had a twin as fine as he was. *Talk about identical, hmmm. I wonder if they're identical all over?* she thought.

Nivea picked up on her surprised expression. *Yeah, bitch, he's a twin, and you won't be getting a double dose of this one.* While the boys embraced, she headed for the kitchen.

Jay picked up on her attitude, but he just blew it off. That was the reason why he hadn't told her that his brother was coming over. He hadn't seen him lately, and he truly missed him, so he figured this would be a good time to talk about his being shot.

CRSO

Von and Trina made themselves comfortable on the love seat portion of the leather, chocolate-and-brown sectional couch, while Nivea and Jay took comfort on the his-and-hers recliners.

Nivea flipped through the channels, looking to find anything to watch as Jay and Von held a conversation about football. She was still upset and wanted them out of her house immediately. As she sat quietly, you could see she was seething with anger. There was fire burning through her veins. She cut her eyes at Von for a split second, trying her best not to stare, but long enough for him to feel the heat.

JayVon should have told me he was having company. Then this fool has the nerve to bring this broad to my home. He is so childish. I hope I find a movie that's midway finished so that Von and his hoodrat can get the hell out.

"Beauty, what are you waiting on? Are you going to put in a movie?"

She stood and walked over to the movie rack. With her back turned, she asked, "What do you all want to watch? We have nothing new up here. Everything is old and we've seen it a million times already. We might as well just buy something on On Demand TV."

Almost in unison, Jay and Von said, "Let's watch *Poetic Justice.*"

Jay said it because he knew that was Von and his favorite. They could watch it a hundred times and still find it funny.

It was also Von's favorite movie, but he'd chosen it just to piss Nivea off even more, thinking of the first time she had come on to him and they'd had sex. She'd started it and now he was going to finish it. He knew bringing Trina over was adding fuel to the fire, but if she wanted to act like shit had never happened between the two of them, then that's what he was going to do— play her game. *By the time I get finished with her ass, she will be begging for my touch.*

Von was hardly ever rejected by a woman, and if she did, after a little persuasion, he had her hooked like a fiend on dope. They always kept coming back for more, so for Nivea to be acting the way she was, had him feeling some type of way. Even if she was his brother's wife, he wasn't letting her off that easy.

"Yeah, Niv, put that movie in. It brings back memories, you feel me?"

Jay watched her for a few seconds, noticing she looked a little flushed in the face. "Beauty, is everything o.k.? Are you feeling sick again?"

Von looked at his brother strangely. "What's wrong with her, bro? Is everything o.k., Niv?"

Before Jay had a chance to tell him she been vomiting a lot lately, Nivea cut him off.

"I'm just fine. I've had a slight headache, nothing to be worried about."

"Yeah, I think that movie would be a great choice." Trina looked from Nivea to Von, then continued. "I don't believe I've ever seen it before. What is it called again? *Po-e-tic Justice,* right?" she asked in her broken English. "I've heard about it, but I've never had the chance to watch it."

If looks could kill, she would have been dead the minute she opened her mouth. *Who asked this retarded-sounding bitch anything?* was what Nivea wanted to say, but instead she gave her the shut-the-hell-up face, then put in the movie, and took her place on her recliner.

By the time they were halfway through the movie, Nivea was so frustrated that she had to get up and go to the bathroom to splash cold water on her face. Every time Trina laughed or wrapped her hands around Von, it irked her nerves. She just had to get out of there before she flipped on everybody, including her husband for inviting them over.

Once she made it to the bathroom and shut the door behind her she let out an aggravated sigh. *Ugggghhhh, fucking idiot, why doesn't he just take his hoe-ass home? He knows this isn't helping the situation with him coming around.* She was so emotional that tears began to fall freely. *I wish I could have them both.* She finally admitted the truth to herself. *Do I have to choose? Yes, it was just sex in the beginning, but now she found herself thinking about a life with him, too. How long can you gone on like this, Nivea?* she questioned herself as she continued to splash water on her face. *I have to let him go; it's only right.*

She emptied her bladder, straightened herself up, and dried up her tears. She forced herself to go back and finish watching the movie; but before she could walk out, Von barged his way in, pushing her back into the bathroom.

"What the hell are you doing?" she whispered. "Von, are you fucking crazy? Are you're trying to get both of us killed?"

"Yeah, you're damn right, I'm crazy. I became that way when I gave you what you were asking for that night, right here in my brother's home, while he lay in the hospital fighting for his life. Now you want to act as if nothing happened?"

"Shhhh, please." She was nervous, but happy, to steal a moment alone with him. The way he hovered over her small frame caused her body to shiver. With Von, there were no limitations. She could ride the wave with him and live life as if nothing in the world mattered as long as he would make her climax over and over again.

"Von, get out and take that ghetto heifer with you."

"Shhh, Niv, I know what you want, what you need. Let me make you feel good." He began to kiss on her neck and massage her swollen breasts.

All the anger and fire she had for him earlier was now pure pleasure. Her love box was where the fire was burning now and needed to be put out. She took long, deep breaths, trying her best to say stop, but nothing came out except for silent moans.

He could feel her damp, moist, needy place as he slid his fingers back and forth. He began to tug on her stretch pants hungrily.

She could tell by the evidence of his arousal he wanted her just as bad as she wanted him. Nivea knew she had to take control, or he would have her bent over on the tub in the next few seconds. Not wanting to, but knowing what was best, she pushed him off her and slapped the taste out of his mouth.

"Leave my damn house and take the trick-of-the-night with you. I told you I was done, and you pull this shit with my husband here? Get out, Von. NOW!'

He stood back, biting his bottom lip.

"It's cool, Niv. Bitches like you make it hard for a nigga to keep it one hundred. First, you trap a nigga by throwing it at me, now you want to play games? I'm cool. I'm out!"

Von left out, grabbed him and Trina some pizza from the kitchen to play it off, then rejoined her and Jay in the living room.

Nivea saw the hurt in his eyes. She felt bad but she didn't know what else to do. *Damnit, should I have stayed in here and let him have his way, while his brother was in the next room? I can't do him like that. That would really be taking it too far.* She was already fighting temptation nightly. She had wanted to call him many a night and meet somewhere, but lying next to her husband stopped her every time. She felt overwhelmed with the emotions of doing what's right or doing what's wrong, and decided not to re-join them. She went upstairs so she could take a long, hot bath and think about what she was going to do with the men in her life.

Chapter Twenty ~ Present Day

Brandy

Brandy called in the next three days and stayed at home, depressed. She missed Robert and her son tremendously, but she had no energy to get up. Rob called her every day, five to ten times, but she sent him straight to voicemail.

She reached on the nightstand to grab a drink and accidentally knocked her purse over. She began to pick up everything that had fallen out and noticed the card that Jay had given her. She looked at the clock, which read four p.m., and wondered if he was busy. She fumbled with the business card for about thirty minutes and decided she would call.

"I hope he isn't busy. I could really use his conversation right about now." Her heart began to beat faster when the phone started to ring.

"Good Deeds Reality. How may I help you?"

She didn't expect a woman to answer the phone, but she remembered his wife's voice on the phone and this woman sounded white. She figured maybe it was his secretary, so she was going to give it a shot.

"Hello? Hellooo?" Stephanie repeated.

"Oh yes, I'm sorry. May I please speak with Mr. Deeds?"

"Sure, may I ask who's calling?"

"I was his nurse, Brandy Carter."

"Oh, of course, you're the wonderful young lady we heard so much about. Let me get him right on line."

"Wow, you finally called."

She could hear the smile in his voice, which put her more at ease. "I see you're back at work. This is a little early, don't you think?"

Jay reclined back in his chair a little and looked out the window. "Actually, it wasn't early enough. If I could have came back the second day out of the hospital, I would have. Anyway, enough about me. How are you doing?"

She sat quietly for a few seconds, breathing through her mouth, which alerted Jay that something was wrong. He instantly became upset, thinking the worse.

"Brandy, what's the matter? Did he hit you again? He heard sniffles. Where are you? Are you safe?"

"No, he didn't hit me again. Lately, I'm the one doing the fighting." She laughed a little, thinking about her getting in a few good jabs on Rob when he was asleep.

"Hey, Brandy, hold on for a second."

Jay stood up, opened his door, and asked Stephanie to hold off all his calls for the next thirty minutes.

"Jay, you didn't have do that."

"It's alright. So tell me what causes a nice lady like you have to fight?"

She began to tell him everything, from her finding the pieces of a condom wrapper in his pocket to the text messages, and every event leading up to her calling him today. He was at a loss for words. He couldn't understand how or why someone as young, smart, and beautiful as she was would put up with such a loser.

"Brandy, you know that I've always kept it real with you, and there will be no difference today. You're taking a chance of losing everything you've worked so hard for. You could be sitting in someone's jail right about now. Your baby-daddy doesn't have anything to lose. You have a son whom you have to take care of.

"If you take him back, that means you'll continue to allow him to do everything he's done in the past, but it will be twice as much now. He's teaching your son to be a loser, just like him. Understand that a real man doesn't sit at home while his wife works. You have to let him go, Brandy. I've told you before, you deserve better, but you have to want better for you and your son."

She listened to him talk as she cried. She was miserable not having man around, even if it was only a piece of a man. Brandy had gotten accustomed to being needed. She'd set her needs aside to help others, and that was how it was in all of her relationships. *Not this time,* she thought. Sick and tired of being used and abused, she decided that she was going to get what she wanted, regardless if it hurt or broke up someone's happy home.

"You know, Jay, I actually feel so much better. I'm not going to take him back; fed-up is an understatement. I'm done. I've been running into this nice guy lately, and every time I see him, I go mute; but I think I'm going to ask him on a date, the next time I run into him. One date won't hurt, right?"

He laughed, playing off his true feelings. He couldn't understand why he felt the way he did, but he almost asked her for the guy's information so he could interview him first.

"That sounds good to me. Just take it slow; right now, you're in a very vulnerable state. You don't want anyone else coming in, tearing you down anymore than what you already are."

"You are a very special man, JayVon. I am glad to have you as a friend," She began to smile on the inside and felt the depression lift off her.

"Likewise, Brandy, likewise. I have to be going, but don't forget to use my number anytime. I don't care what time of the day it is. Before he realized what he was saying, he said, "In fact, here's my cell phone number."

After she hung up the phone, she looked through her closet for something sexy to wear out to the club. She remembered Coco telling her the name of the club where Von normally chilled!

CRSO

Brandy skipped the club and decided just call Von. She told him straight up that she wanted sex, and he didn't hesitate to take her up on her offer. Now, after parking her car at his place, the two were on their way to motel not too far from Von's place. Brandy was anxious to finally get a taste of that good dick that Coco bragged about so much. She was excited to feel like she would finally be paying Rob back, but she was also a little nervous.

CRSO

Von

"She needs to stop playing and keep that shit real," Von blurted.

"Huh?" Brandy looked at him confused

Von looked over at her and shook his head. "Come on, get out."

He got out of the car and stood waiting for Brandy. As he waited for Brandy to walk around to his side of the car, he pretended he didn't see Nivea's black-on-black Rover pull into the motel lot. Von quickly grabbed Brandy by the hand and walked toward the room.

"Don't we have to pay?" Brandy asked.

Von ignored her question and continued to walk to room 106. As soon as he put his hand on the knob, a buzzer went off, and Von turned the knob to open the door. He looked at a puzzled Brandy and winked his eye.

CRSO

Nivea

Nivea, stop with this foolishness. You have a husband at home who loves you dearly. Her conscience began to lecture her, and she slowed her pace, but she never stopped walking toward Von and his chick. The closer she got, the more upset she became. *How dare him!*

Enough with this madness! Your husband loves and takes care of you. You are going to lose him. That was so true. Jay did love her, and if he ever found out about them, he would probably kill them both.

But she had come too far to go back. She was there, and she wanted to know what in the hell was going on, who was he with. Von and the chick were now standing in front of the room. When Nivea saw Von open the door, she began to lightly jog their way. Von saw Nivea coming, and pulled Brandy into his arms and kissed her.

Nivea became outraged. *What in the hell is she doing with my man? Did I just say "my?" Yes, I did.*

"TrayVon, what in the hell is your problem, and who in the fuck is this?" Nivea looked at woman he was with, and her expression went from angry to surprised when she recognized who it was. "The fucking nurse?" She turned up her nose and looked Brandy up and down as if she was disgusted. Nivea then looked at Von. "Like really, Von?" She chuckled. "If you don't send this tired, thirsty bitch home and now . . ." She put her hands on her hips.

Brandy stepped back and gave Nivea a once-over. "Excuse you. You're calling somebody thirsty, and you're the one following a man to a motel, jumping out, acting all crazy? Wait, and don't you have a man? Are you trying to get a double dose? Isn't your husband—"

Before Brandy could finish her sentence, Nivea charged at her and grabbed her hair. Just as Von was pulling Nivea off Brandy, Brandy punched her in the side of the face. Von stepped between them.

"Brandy, go home. I'll call you later."

Brandy looked at him with her eyebrows up.

"Just go."

He reached in his pocket, pulled out a stack, pulled three twenties off, and tried to hand them to Brandy.

"Nigga, I don't need you or your money." She looked over at Nivea, who was standing there with her arms folded as if she had won the battle. "Bitch, this ain't over. I will have the last laugh."

She walked off, oblivious to how she would get home. Brandy stood in front of the hotel lobby, deciding whether she should chance walking back to Von's place to retrieve her car, or should she call a cab. *But I have no money on my card until Friday,* she thought. Brandy looked in her purse to see if she had any loose bills; when she didn't find any, she gave up and began to walk. *I promise I will get their asses back.*

With tears running down her face, she pulled out her cell. She dialed the number and waited for him to pick up,

"Hello," he answered, sounding fully alert.

"JayVon, I'm sorry to call, but I need to tell you something?"

"Brandy, are you o.k.? Did he hit you?"

"No, I'm fine, and I am not calling about Rob. I'm calling about your wife."

ଔଛ

Coco

"What's up, ma?" he answered the call.

Coco smiled. "Hey, you, I was just calling to let you know that I am on the way." Coco took a right onto the freeway on-ramp.

"Alright, I'll be there in a minute. I'll hit you up when I get there."

"Alright. I'll text you the room number."

"Later." He and Coco ended the call.

As Coco was driving to the hotel, the palms of her hands got sweaty. She couldn't believe that she was about to take it there. She knew the consequences, but she thought, *fuck it*. She wasn't trying to get involved in a relationship. All she wanted was someone to talk to, cuddle with, and if she decided to take it there, that was what she would do. But he wasn't like that. They'd kicked it a few times before, and he'd never tried anything with her.

Coco exited the freeway and made a right at the first corner. When she passed a thick girl with *Poetic Justice* braids, she did a double take. *That look like Brandy,* she thought as she looked through her rearview mirror. She knew it wasn't. For one, Brandy has a car, and two, she wouldn't be over on this side of town.

Coco turned into the hotel parking lot and pulled into registration parking. She grabbed her purse and got out of the car. As she was walking to the window, she began to get butterflies in her stomach. She always got like that when she got ready to see him.

"Hi, a room for the night please?" she told the hotel attendant. After showing her ID, filling out the registration form, and paying for the room, she got the room keys and walked back to her car. *Room 107,* she texted him, then went to park closer to the rooms. Coco parked, and grabbed her overnight bag and purse. She got out of the car, shut the door, and hit the alarm. She looked over at the row and spotted room 107. In midstride to the room, she stopped and turned back around. She had forgotten the drink. Coco pulled her keys from her purse and popped her trunk.

Her heart dropped, and she immediately got an instant headache. "I know the fuck that isn't Von's truck." She stared at the vehicle and quickly walked over to it. Coco looked at the rims. She then walked back and looked at the license plate. She took a deep breath. "This muthafucka!" She walked over to the passenger side, and when she looked through the window, she saw a picture of him and her son on the dashboard.

Totally forgetting that she was also at the motel, ready to be up to no good, Coco went into beast mode. Pow! She kicked the car with her stiletto. "Von, bring your bitch-ass out of there and now. Pow! She kicked the car again. "I swear on my son that I will tear this muthafucka up." She looked behind her and saw someone peep out of the window. "Bitch, I see you," she fumed, as she made her way to the door.

The pump stopped at fifty dollars and seven cents. Travis walked back into the station to get his change. He couldn't get her off his mind. He didn't know if he was infatuated with the fact that he was getting something that he wasn't supposed to have, or the fact that she was sexier than a muthafucka, and he was finally about to take it there.

"Let me get a pack of Magnums," he told the attendant and tossed him a twenty. "Make that two packs."

Trav grabbed his change and the condoms. As he stepped out of the station door, he checked his surroundings. Besides the car at the air pump, the gas station was clear. Before getting into his car, Travis pulled his cell from his pocket and checked his text. *Cool,* he texted back and then hopped in the truck. "You're one cold-ass nigga."

He laughed as he slammed his car door. Just as he started the truck, he felt a cold piece of steal placed in the back of his head.

"Nigga, don't move," the intruder warned. As if he'd read Travis' mind, he added, "I've got your shit," he said, referring to the gun Travis had left on the seat.

"The boss wants to see you; you know where to go."

"What are you talking about? I ain't got no boss, nigga?" Trav heard a button being pressed on the phone.

"Now repeat what you said," said the intruder.

"I ain't got no boss," Travis repeated.

"You might be right. Unless you tell me what happened that fucking night, your ass is as good as dead," the man on the other end of the phone barked.

Damn! He caught me slipping.....

To be continued....

Checkout ABL's Bestsellers

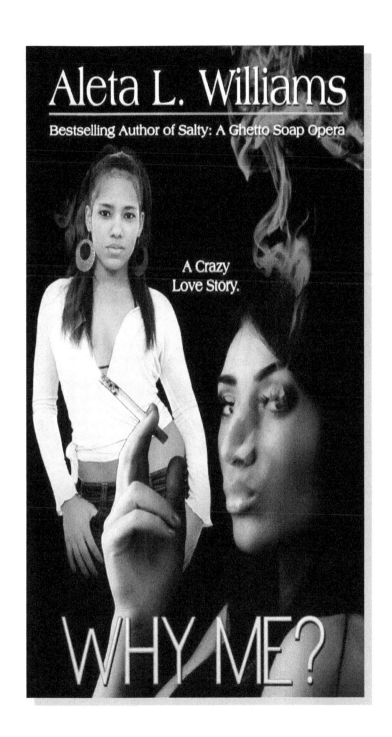

Why
HER?
THE SEQUEL TO WHY ME?

ALETA L. WILLIAMS
BESTSELLING AUTHOR OF WHY ME & THE SALTY SERIES

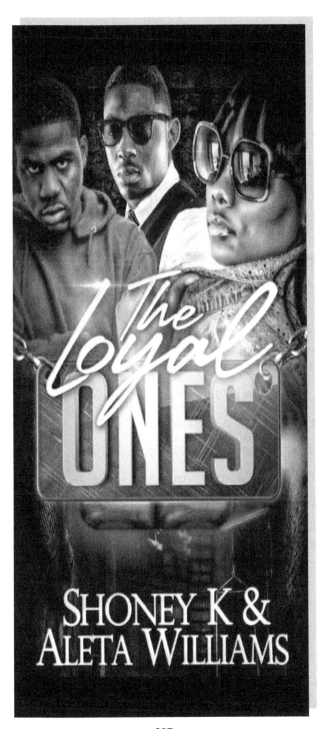

~ **Apryl**

Before I give my shout outs, I must say this: Growing up, I suffered with believing the negativity that was spoken in my ear and over my life—that I was dumb and I couldn't spell worth nothing. Over the years, the more I couldn't spell, the more I doubted myself.

"But, God!" Once I made up in my mind to trust in the Lord, things started happening. I was twenty-seven when He changed my life. I went back to school and started studying for my GED. In less than five months, they were saying, "Apryl, you're ready to take your test." God stepped in again and made it where, any time I took a test, I got double the time, so I had more time to focus. Then God said, "Don't worry about your scores. Go sign up for college." Not knowing if I had passed or not, I went to sign up for college and took the placement test. A couple days later, I got a phone call from my teacher. She said, "Apryl, come and pick up your cap and gown. You passed." Lord that was you!

That started it off. I went to college the Lord helped me to make a 3.5 GPA—the same girl who couldn't spell and was called dumb. But, He didn't stop there! I got a job with Bells Caring Services, as a supported living coach, helping to place people with disabilities in homes, teaching them how to live on their own and how to pay their own bills. With the paperwork that was involved I thought I couldn't do it. ***"But, God!"***

And to answer the question that everybody wants to know: How did Apryl start writing? Is this my passion? No! This was another way of God showing me that I can do all things through Him. I've learned that there are seeds planted on the inside of us, but it takes us to water them so they can grow. God has already given all of us gifts and talents; the rest is up us.

I started writing a few years ago and never finished, but God said it was time. He placed the right people in my path to make it happen. He also sent confirmation through Mother Emma, Rest in Peace. But before she passed away, she said, "Apryl, I had a dream about you last night." I'm like, "About me? What happened?" She said, "You were at your book signing." I was like, "No, that can't be me. She must be talking about my friend." Well, mother it is coming to pass. Not only did I write it, I wrote it all from my cell phone. And guess what y'all? I still can't spell that well. LOL. But I know that I know that I know what His ability is. ***All glory to God.*** Once again, Lord, I just thank You because now I know that I can!

To my Daddy, Reverend Tyson, and his wife, Gladys Tyson; Nelson; my sisters—Evonne, Gloria, and Emma; my brothers— Jimmy, Chris, James, and Clifford; cousins Tisha and Man; my nieces and nephews; Aunt Hattie B.; Rest in Peace—Godmother

Liz and Auntie Hat!—I miss y'all; Momma Linda and husband, Fred; to my pastor, Tom Jones, and first lady, Williemay, and my entire church family: I love you all and thank you for the support.

TO MY BFF's: THIS IS THE FUN PART - LOL

Michelle, when I think about you, I think about the time when we were younger and I ate a piece of bubble gum out of your mouth. LOL. Life sisters . . .

Gordy, when I think about you, I think about the time when we were younger, but grown children. Lol. I came over to your house, and we were on that balcony early in the morning singing, *God Is a Good God.* Taking it way back. LOL

Brandy, when I think about you, I think about us not even waking the children up, but grabbing all four of them at three in the morning, running outside, and jumping in the pool with them without warning. #fun LOL

Samantha, My PT as I call you. When I think about you, I think about you and I having a nickname for everyone, then accidentally slipping up and calling that one guy we named "Goodjuug." That mess was funny. In our getting voices . . . LOL

Maribell, when I think of you, I think about when we met up for drinks, and we had one too many. The guy sitting across from us had his girlfriend with him, but he kept looking at me, and you went off. Waaaay too funny. I had to get you out of there. LOL

Aleta, when I think about you, I think about the first time we met in Atlanta, Georgia. You came and picked me up from the hotel. When I got in the backseat, a Charlie horse cramped up my stomach, and I had to jump out. You were in the car laughing at me. LMBO

Evonne, When I think about you, I think about that training class!!!! You know, so get ready; bring apple. Lol

LOL. You, ladies, all hold a special place in my heart. I love you guys so much, and I'm so glad to be able to call you all my sisters. Thank you for your encouragement.

To my husband: What's taking you so long? God hasn't finished molding you yet? Lol, but I see ya from afar!

To the founder of ABL, Author Aleta Williams, thank you for seeing in me what I didn't want to see in myself. I thank God for you more than you can imagine. ABL is blessed, and that's how I know this was God's doing, the way it all came about. Thanks for being obedient to God when He said to push me, and for staying home to pull through all of my mess. Thank you to the editor, Mrs.

Gloria Palmer, you have a sweet spirit. I know you do love your job, but it couldn't be me. LOL

And to all my friends and fans: Thank you in advance for your love and support. A&A is in the building. Stand up! God bless. ~ **Apryl**

***

~ Aleta

Shout Out: To the entire Salty family and to all those who have supported me along the way. I pray God's richest blessings over your life.

~Aleta L Williams